Edwin W. (Edwin Wilbur) Rice

**Hymnal for Primary Classes**

A Collection of Hymns and Tunes, Recitations, and Exercisess

Edwin W. (Edwin Wilbur) Rice

**Hymnal for Primary Classes**
*A Collection of Hymns and Tunes, Recitations, and Exercisess*

ISBN/EAN: 9783337089740

Printed in Europe, USA, Canada, Australia, Japan

Cover: Foto ©Thomas Meinert / pixelio.de

More available books at **www.hansebooks.com**

# HYMNAL FOR PRIMARY CLASSES.

A COLLECTION OF

Hymns and Tunes, Recitations, and Exercises,

BEING A

## MANUAL FOR PRIMARY SUNDAY-SCHOOLS.

---

COMPILED BY A TEACHER

OF MANY YEARS' EXPERIENCE.

---

WORD EDITION.

---

PHILADELPHIA:
THE AMERICAN SUNDAY-SCHOOL UNION,
1122 CHESTNUT STREET.

NEW YORK BRANCH: 111 FIFTH AVENUE.

# PUBLISHER'S PREFACE.

THIS Hymnal and Manual is the fruit of many years of painstaking and successful experience in Primary Class teaching. The process of sifting, selecting, composing and arranging the hymns and tunes has gone on slowly, by subjecting the pieces and exercises generally to the test of actual and prolonged use in a large Primary School.

The original purpose, therefore, was not "to make a book for publication," but to bring together a choice selection of the best hymns, Scriptural truths and exercises that proved most suitable and helpful in personal work among Primary Classes.

A guiding purpose in making the selection was to have every hymn and exercise teach the love of Jesus, some Scriptural truth, some important moral principle, which, when once fixed in the minds of children, might ever influence their lives.

The material has been patiently gleaned from all available sources, without stint of cost or time. Many of the hymns and tunes are original, and have never before been published. This music is written especially to suit young children's voices, and is not arranged for four-part singing, but is to be sung in unison. The harmony is arranged as a pleasing accompaniment to aid in holding the attention of children.

To promote a true spirit of reverence in the Sunday-school and its services, it is suggested that before prayer the children rise, clasp their hands, bow their heads, and repeat after the leader the words of the prayer. This has long been tried and found effective.

The hymns, tunes and exercises in this work are copyrighted, and should not be reprinted except by written permission of the publishers. Thanks are due to many composers, hymn writers and publishers for kindly granting permission to use selections from their works. Particular acknowledgments are given throughout the book.

The Manual containing questions, answers, and simple prayers and orders of service should prove an important aid to Primary Class teachers, in their high and holy work.

EDWIN W. RICE.

☞ WARNING.—As many of the hymns, recitations, etc., are copyrighted, they cannot be reprinted unless permission is received from owners.

# HYMNAL FOR PRIMARY CLASSES.

**1.**

Holy Bible! book divine!
Precious treasure! thou art mine!
Mine, to tell me whence I came;
Mine, to teach me what I am.

Cho.—Holy Bible! book divine!
Precious treasure! thou art mine!

Mine art thou to guide my feet;
Mine to judge, condemn, acquit;
Mine, to show a Saviour's love;
Mine, to chide me when I rove.

Mine, to tell of joys to come,
And the rebel sinner's doom;
Mine, to show by living faith,
Man can triumph over death.

**2.**

Precious Bible! how I love thee,
  Thy sweet truth is my delight;
Like the rays of Heaven's sunshine,
  Thou art many a pathway's light.
Infant lips thy truths have whisper'd,
  Infant voices sung thy praise;
Gracious blessings cheer us onward,
  As we walk in wisdom's ways.

In the homes of rich and lowly,
  In far distant lands and climes;
Where God's people meet to worship,
  Call'd by ringing Sabbath chimes;
There we find thy precious precepts,
  As reveal'd by God to man;
Gracious news of our redemption,
  And of Calv'ry's wondrous plan.

Heathen nations long in darkness,
  Now behold the promised light;
As they seek thy hidden treasures,
  Found within each page so bright.
Book of promise! psalm of praises!
  Light and life to wand'rers given;
Be with us while life is passing,
  Guide our footsteps up to Heav'n.

---

**3.**

We'll not give up the Bible,
  God's holy Book of truth;
The blessed staff of hoary age,
  The guide of early youth;

The sun that sheds a glorious light
    O'er every dreary road,
The voice that speaks a Saviour's love
    And calls us home to God.

Cho.—We'll not give up the Bible,
    God's holy Book of truth;
The blessed staff of hoary age,
    The guide of early youth.

We'll not give up the Bible,
    For pleasure or for pain;
We'll buy the truth, and sell it not,
    For all that we might gain.
Though man should try to take our prize
    By guile, or cruel might,
We'll suffer all that man could do,
    And, God defend the right.

We'll not give up the Bible,
    But spread it far and wide;
Until its saving voice be heard
    Beyond the rolling tide;
'Till all shall know its gracious pow'r,
    And with one voice and heart,
Resolve that from God's sacred word,
    We'll never, never part.

---

**4.**

Who made the sky so bright and blue?
    Who made the fields so green?
Who made the flow'rs that smell so sweet,
    In pretty colors green?

Answer:—

'Twas God our Father and our King;
Oh, let us all His praises sing.

Who made the birds to soar so high,
    And taught them how to sing?
Who made the pretty butterfly,
    And painted her bright wing?

Who made the sun that shines so bright,
    And gladdens all we see,
Which comes to give us light and heat,
    That happy we may be?

Who made the moon and stars so high,
    The darksome night to cheer,
That shine so bright in yonder sky,
    Oft as the heav'ns are clear?

---

**5.**

As the buds their leaves unfolding,
    Tender buds that early bloom,
Looking up to meet the sunshine,
    Waft to God their sweet perfume;
So may we in life's bright springtime
    Hearty thanks to Jesus give,
Sending forth in pure devotion
    Sweetest praises while we live.

As the buds are trained and cultured,
    By a skillful loving hand,
May our hearts be trained for Jesus,
    And a fairer, brighter land;
Thus remembering our Creator,
    In the spring and morn of youth,
We may yet unfold our blossoms
    At the fount of Life and Truth.

Copyright, 1883, by Biglow & Main, used by permission.

## PRIMARY CLASSES.

**6.**

THE pretty flow'rs have come again,
    The roses and the daisies;
And from the trees, oh, hear how plain
    The birds are singing praises!

CHO.—How charming now our walks will be,
    By meadows full of clover,
Thro' shady lanes, where we can see
    The branches bending over.

The flow'rs are blooming fresh and bright
    In just the same old places;
And oh, it fills me with delight
    To see their charming faces.

The air is sweet, the sky is blue,
    The woods with songs are ringing;
And I'm so happy, that I, too,
    Can hardly keep from singing.

---

**7.**

LIFTING up each chalice bright,
    Buttercups and daisies;
In the grand and joyous light,
    Buttercups and daisies;
We love your bonny eyes to greet,
That smile so fondly at our feet,
For then fair Spring and Summer meet—
    Buttercups and daisies.

King and Queen among the flow'rs!
    Buttercups and daisies;
How you gild the noontide hours!
    Buttercups and daisies;
And when your simple charms you wield,
Just like an army on the field;
Oh! then what joy your blossoms yield!
    Buttercups and daisies.

**8.**

All over the valleys so green and fair,
  The lily buds soft are sleeping;
He spoke through the rays of the sun, and lo!
  The lily buds forth came peeping.

Chorus:—
  He sprinkled the rain from His great white cloud,
    He scattered the dew on the clover;
  He painted the lilies by brooks that flow
    All over the meadows, and over.

  He cares for the lily, and cares for me,
    His love will forsake me never;
  The mercy that foldeth the evening flower,
    Will tenderly shield me ever.

Copyright, 1883, by Biglow & Main, used by permission.

---

**9.**

Summer days are coming, coming,
  Smiling o'er the hills;
Ev'ry little brook that ripples,
  Some sweet task fulfills;
So may we, some duty finding
  Still in joy or song,
Make some pathway greener, brighter,
  As we pass along.

Cho.—Summer days are coming,
  Smiling o'er the hills;
Ev'ry little brook that ripples,
  Some sweet task fulfills.

Copyright, 1883, by Biglow & Main, used by permission.

**10.**

It is God's mercy gives us
  The sunshine and the rain,
That paints in verdant beauty
  The mountain and the plain.

By Him were all things fashioned
  Around us and afar;
He made the earth and ocean,
  And ev'ry shining star.

He made the pleasant Springtime,
  The Summer bright and warm,
The golden days of Autumn,
  The Winter and the storm.

He makes the glorious sunset,
  The moon to sail on high;
He bids the breezes fan us
  And thunder clouds to fly.

He gives us ev'ry blessing,
  To Him our lives we owe;
He sent His Son to save us
  From sin and death and woe.

---

**11.**

I sing the mighty power of God,
  That made the mountains rise;
That spread the flowing seas abroad,
  And built the lofty skies.

I sing the wisdom that ordained
  The sun to rule the day;
The moon shines full at His command,
  And all the stars obey.

I sing the goodness of the Lord,
    That filled the earth with food;
He formed the creatures with His word
    And then pronounced them good.

There's not a plant or flower below
    But makes His glories known;
And clouds arise and tempests blow
    By order from His throne.

---

**12.**

I OUGHT to be a happy child,
    For little though I be,
I have a Friend who loves me so,
    He even died for me.
But though He lives in heaven so high,
    That seems so far away;
Yet from His throne above the sky
    He smiles on me to-day.

CHO.—I ought to be a happy child,
    For little though I be,
I have a Friend who loves me so,
    He even died for me.

He guides me all the way that leads,
    To Canaan's happy land;
And I shall never lose the road,
    Whilst Jesus holds my hand.
Oh, yes, I am a happy child,
    For little though I be,
I have a Friend who loves me so,
    He even died for me.

**13.**

O sing to me of Jesus
  And of His dying love;
Sing how He came to save us,
  And raise our souls above.
Sing of the great salvation,
  He purchased on the tree;
Oh, glorious welcome tidings,
  He died for you and me.

He left the starry mansions,
  His Father's home on high,
And came to earth to seek us,
  While doom'd in sin to die.
Oh, tell the wondrous story,
  How Jesus came to save;
And wretched, guilty sinners,
  To ransom from the grave.

Ye children bow and worship,
  With angels sing His praise;
And sound aloud the anthems,
  Of his redeeming grace.
O sing to me of Jesus,
  Tell His amazing love;
He came to earth to save us,
  And raise our souls above.

---

**14.**

Only little children,
  Yet the Saviour knows
All our little sorrows,
  All our childish woes;

Knows that we are helpless,
  Frail and sinful too;
Knows if we have striven,
  To be good and true.

Only little children,
  Yet the Saviour hears,
When the children tell Him,
  All their hopes and fears;
Hears our songs of praises,
  As to Him we sing;
Though He lives in heaven,
  As our Lord and King.

Only little children,
  Yet the Saviour said,
When He laid His hands in
  Blessing on their head,
Suffer little children,
  Unto me to come;
There are many like them,
  In my Father's home.

Only little children,
  Do not us despise;
Only come and help us,
  To be good and wise.
More like gentle Jesus,
  Father, let us be
Till we rest forever,
  Jesus Lord, with thee.

**15.**
How loving is Jesus who came from the sky,
In tenderest pity for sinners to die;
His hands and His feet were nailed to the tree,
And all this He suffered for you and for me.

How gladly does Jesus, free pardon impart,
To all who receive Him by faith in the heart,
No evil befalls them, their home is above,
And Jesus throws round them, the arms of His love.

How precious is Jesus to all who believe,
And out of His fullness what grace they receive,
When weak He supports them, when erring He guides,
And ev'rything needful, He kindly provides.

O, give them to Jesus your earliest days,
They only are happy who walk in His ways;
In life and in death, He will still be your friend,
For whom Jesus once loves, He loves to the end.

---

**16.**

There's a Friend for little children
   Above the bright blue sky,
A Friend that never changes,
   Whose love will never die.
Unlike our friends by nature,
   Who change with changing years;
The Friend is always worthy
   The precious name He bears.

There's a rest for little children
   Above the bright blue sky,
Who love the blessed Saviour,
   And Abba, Father cry.
A rest from every trouble,
   From sin and danger free,
Where every little pilgrim
   Shall rest eternally.

There's a home for little children
    Above the bright blue sky,
Where Jesus reigns in glory,
    A home of peace and joy.
No home on earth is like it,
    Nor can with it compare,
For every one is happy,
    Nor can be happier there.

There's a crown for little children
    Above the bright blue sky,
And all who look to Jesus,
    Shall wear it by and by:
A crown of brightest glory,
    Which He shall sure bestow,
On all who love the Saviour
    And walk with Him below.

---

## 17.

'Tis wonderful love in Christ we see,
The love of God for you and me;
Love which shines free as the sun's bright rays,
And wonderful too, in all its ways.

CHORUS:—
    Do you know? Do you know?
    Know of this wonderful love to man?
    Do you know? Do you know?
    Know of this wonderful love?

This wonderful love to our fallen race,
Who can its measures fitly trace?
For down from His home the Saviour came,
To bleed and die on the cross of shame.

High as the Heaven extends above,
So is the height of this great love;
The love which the Father has bestowed,
That we should be called the sons of God.

Copyright, 1883, by Biglow & Main, used by permission.

---

**18.**

SOFTLY sing the love of Jesus!
　For our hearts are full of tears,
As we think how, walking humbly
　This low earth for weary years,
Without riches, without dwelling,
　Wounded sore by foe and friend,
In the garden, and in dying,
　Jesus loved us to the end!

Gladly sing the love of Jesus!
　Let us lean upon His arm,
If He loves us, what can grieve us?
　If He keeps us, what can harm?
Still He lays His hands in blessing
　On each timid little face,
And in heaven the children's angels
　Near the throne have always place.

Ever sing the love of Jesus!
　Let the day be dark or clear,
Ev'ry pain and ev'ry sorrow
　Bring Him to His own more near,
Death's cold wave need not affright us,
　When we know that He has died,
When we see the face of Jesus
　Smiling from the other side!

**19.**

    THEY crowned our Saviour's brow with thorns,
      They pierced and made it bleed;
  And not content they mocked Him then,
    And struck Him with a reed.

REFRAIN :—
    Oh, what a kind, forgiving Lord,
      Such cruel pain to bear,
  That we who trust Him as we ought,
    A crown of life might wear!

    Our hands shall gather roses sweet
      For Him our Saviour King,
  And gladly in our Sabbath home,
    We'll crown Him while we sing.

    He trod for us a thorny path;
      He died for you and me;
  Our love, the purest we can give,
    That rosy crown shall be.

Copyright, 1882, by H. P. Main. Used by per.

---

**20.**

    ONE there is above all others
      Well deserves the name of Friend;
  His is love beyond a brother's,
    Costly, free, and knows no end.
  Which of all our friends, to save us,
    Could or would have shed his blood?
  But this Saviour died to have us
    Reconciled, in Him, to God.

When He lived on earth abased,
    Friend of sinners was His name;
Now, above all glory raised,
    He rejoices in the same.
Oh, for grace our hearts to soften!
    Teach us, Lord, at length to love;
We, alas, forget too often
    What a Friend we have above.

---

**21.**

How precious is the story
    Of our Redeemer's birth,
Who left the realms of glory,
    And came to dwell on earth!
He saw our sad condition,
    Our guilt, and sin, and shame;
To save us from perdition.
    The blessed Jesus came.

He came to earth from heaven,
    To weep, and bleed, and die,
That we might be forgiven,
    And raised to God on high.
His kindness and compassion
    To children then were shown;
The heirs of His salvation,
    He claimed them for His own.

Oh, may I love this Saviour,
    So good, so kind, so mild!
And may I find His favor,
    A young but sinful child;
And in His blissful heaven
    May I at last appear,
With all my sins forgiven,
    To know and praise him there.

**22.**

I THINK when I read that sweet story of old,
  When Jesus was here among men,
How He called little children as lambs to His fold,
  I should like to have been with them then.
I wish that His hands had been placed on my head,
  That His arm had been thrown around me,
And that I might have seen His kind look when He said,
  "Let the little ones come unto Me."

Yet still to His footstool in prayer I may go,
  And ask for a share in His love,
And if I thus earnestly seek Him below,
  I shall see Him and hear Him above;
In that beautiful place He is gone to prepare
  For all who are washed and forgiven;
And many dear children are gathering there,
  "For of such is the kingdom of heaven."

---

**23.**

  ALAS! and did my Saviour bleed,
    And did my Sovereign die,
  Would He devote that sacred head
    For such a worm as I?

  Was it for crimes that I had done
    He groaned upon the tree?
  Amazing pity! grace unknown!
    And love beyond degree!

Well might the sun in darkness hide,
    And shut His glories in,
When God the mighty Maker died
    For man the creature's sin.

Thus might I hide my blushing face
    While His dear cross appears,
Dissolve my heart in thankfulness,
    And melt mine eyes to tears.

But drops of grief can ne'er repay
    The debt of love I owe;
Here, Lord, I give myself away,—
    'Tis all that I can do.

---

**24.**

Jesus loves me! this I know,
For the Bible tells me so;
Little ones to Him belong,
They are weak but He is strong.

CHORUS:—Yes, Jesus loves me,
    Yes, Jesus loves me,
    Yes, Jesus loves me,
        The Bible tells me so.

Jesus loves me! He will stay,
Close beside me, all the way;
If I love Him, when I die
He will take me home on high.

Jesus loves me! He who died,
Heaven's gate to open wide;
He will wash away my sin,
Let His little child come in.

Jesus loves me! loves me still,
Tho' I'm very weak and ill;
From His shining throne on high,
Comes to watch me where I lie.

Copyright, 1883, by Biglow & Main, used by permission.

---

**25.   Questions and Answers.**

QUES.—Who came from heaven to ransom me?
ANS.—Jesus, who died upon the tree.
QUES.—Why did He come from heaven above?
ANS.—He came because His name was Love.
QUES.—And did He die—the Son of God?
ANS.—Yes, on the cross, He shed His blood.
QUES.—Why did my Lord and Saviour bleed?
ANS.—That we from evil might be freed.
QUES.—When He had died, what happened then?
ANS.—On the third day He rose again.
QUES.—Where did He go, when He had risen?
ANS.—He went to God's right hand in heaven.
QUES.—Where is He now? Is He still there?
ANS.—Yes, and He pleads with God in prayer.
QUES.—What does He pray for, and for whom?
ANS.—He prays, that we to Him, might come.
QUES.—Should we not come? Should we not come?
ANS.—Oh, yes, Christ is the sinner's home.
QUES.—Christ is the weary sinner's home!
ANS.—Oh, let us come! Oh, let us come!

**26.**

It is not far to Jesus,
  If you only knew how near,
You would reach Him in a moment,
  And banish all your fear.
He is standing close beside you,
  If only you could see,
And saying,—could you hear Him,
  "Let the children come to me!"

Cho.—It is not far to Jesus,
  If you only knew how near,
You would reach Him in a moment,
  And banish all your fear.

You know He never changes,
  As your little friends do here?
He is always kind and ready,
  To comfort and to cheer.
It matters not how little,
  How very young or weak;
And if you have been sinful,
  It was you He came to seek.

You really must love Jesus,
  When you think of all His love;
In coming down from heaven,
  That happy home above.
And lying in a manger,
  And suffering so much woe;
That you and all dear children,
  To that bright world might go.

**27.**

HARK! I hear the Saviour calling:
"Little children, come to me;
I will bless you, save you, keep you,
I from sin will set you free."

CHO.—He calls again: O let us, then,
With one united cry,
The call obey, and humbly say—
"Dear Jesus, here am I."

"Come," says Jesus, "in the morning
Of your bright and tender youth;
I will be your guide and helper,
I'm the Way, the Life, the Truth."

"Come without a moment's waiting,
In your want and weakness come;
I will take you, I will love you,
I will bring you to my home."

"Come, for 'twas to seek and save you,
I to earth from heaven came down;
Come, that I may have and hold you
In my everlasting crown."

"Come, there's nothing now to hinder,
Little child who e'er thou art;
I for thee myself have given;
Give me back thyself—thy heart."

By permission of Asa Hull, owner of Copyright.

**28.**

Come to Jesus, come to Jesus,
  Come to Jesus to-day;
To-day come to Jesus,
  Come to Jesus to-day.

He will save you, He will save you,
  He will save you to-day;
To-day He will save you,
  He will save you to-day.

Don't reject Him, don't reject Him,
  Don't reject Him to-day;
To-day don't reject Him,
  Don't reject Him to-day.

He is ready, He is ready,
  He is ready to-day;
To-day He is ready,
  He is ready to-day.

Oh, believe Him, oh, believe Him,
  Oh, believe Him to-day;
To-day, oh, believe Him,
  Oh, believe Him to-day.

Do not tarry, do not tarry,
  Do not tarry to-day;
To-day do not tarry,
  Do not tarry to-day.

Hallelujah, hallelujah,
  Hallelujah, Amen;
Amen, hallelujah,
  Hallelujah, Amen.

  The words *just now* can be used for *to-day*.

1. "Come unto me, all ye that labor and are heavy laden, and I will give you rest."—MATT. 11: 28.

   *Chorus.*—Come to Jesus.

2. "Believe on the Lord Jesus Christ, and thou shalt be saved."—ACTS 16: 31.

   *Chorus.*—He will save you.

3. "God so loved the world, that he gave his only begotten Son, that whosoever believeth in him should not perish, but have everlasting life."—JOHN 3: 16.

   *Chorus.*—Oh, believe Him.

4. "Him that cometh to me I will in no wise cast out."—JOHN 6: 37.

   *Chorus.*—He'll receive you.

5. "The blood of Jesus Christ his Son cleanseth us from all sin."—1 JOHN 1: 7.

   *Chorus.*—He will cleanse you.

6. "Greater love hath no man than this, that a man lay down his life for his friends."—JOHN 15: 13.

   *Chorus.*—Jesus loves you.

7. He is waiting, etc.
8. He'll forgive you, etc.
9. He'll renew you, etc.
10. Hallelujah, Amen, etc.

**29.**

    Oh, many, many children
      In Zion shall be found;
    We hear their happy voices,
      And pleasant is the sound;
    For children can be Christians,
      And while at work, or play,
    Be gentle like the Master,
      And all His words obey.

CHORUS.—Oh, children, come to Jesus!
      His service is a joy;
    Oh, come within the city,
      Yes, ev'ry girl and boy.

    Oh, who will be the children
      Within the city bright?
    Will you be one to enter,
      And come by morning light?
    Oh, do not wait till older—
      The shadows may appear—
    You may not see to enter
      When night is almost here.

    Then come and bring a playmate,
      Perchance a brother dear;
    Let sisters come together,
      Oh, never, never fear;
    For Zion must have children
      Upon her golden street,
    Then come, and bring in with you
      Whoever you may meet.

From Infant Praises by per. of John J. Hood.

**30.**

What tender words! how sweet a voice!
'Tis Christ the Lord who speaks:
"Come unto Me, come and rejoice,
The child shall find, who seeks."

"Come unto Me, with words of prayer,
With trusting hearts, oh, come!
I'll make your souls my loving care,
To heaven I'll lead you home."

"There many mansions waiting stand,
Prepared for those I love;
Oh, child, give Me thy trusting hand,
Then dwell with Me above."

Blest is the child, whose youthful heart
Shall hear the Saviour's call;
And choosing now the better part,
Escape sin's bitter thrall.

Thro' earth's dark way he'll safely pass,
Held by that blessed hand;
And, shouting victory at last,
Reach heaven's thrice happy land.

---

**31.**

Jesus' voice my name is calling,
Seeks my heart to win;
Hardened is my heart with sinning,
Shall I let Him in?

Shall I hear His tender pleading—
  Can I tell Him nay?
Can I close the door upon Him,
  See Him turn away?

REFRAIN:—
Hark, I hear my Saviour gently knocking, knocking—
While with fear my guilty heart is throbbing, throbbing;
Jesus stands without it, gently knocking, knocking—
Christ, my Saviour, knocking at the door.

  Patiently the Lord is waiting,
    Waiting at the door;
  Pierced for me the hand that's knocking,
    Knocking ever more.
  Wide the door with joy I'll open,
    Bid the Lord come in!
  In my heart forever dwelling,
    Casting out my sin.

REFRAIN:—
I will open to His gentle knocking, knocking—
While with joy my gladdened heart is throbbing, throbbing;
Jesus stands without, no longer knocking, knocking—
Christ, my Saviour, enters at the door.

Used by permission of Dr. H. R. Palmer, owner of the copyright.

---

**32.**

  Jesus is knocking at the door,
  I know He oft has knocked before;
  And now He comes this blessed day,
  I must invite Him in to stay.

I think I would let Jesus in,
But He will find so much of sin;
I fear He will not love to stay,
What shall I do, say yea, or nay?

Say yes, my child, and open wide
The door, that He may here abide;
He'll cleanse your heart from self and sin,
And keep it too, all pure and clean.

He'll make His home within your soul,
And ev'ry thought and wish control;
You will be happy, little one,
When Jesus Christ your heart has won.

*(For last verse only; rise at singing.)*

I will! I will! come, Jesus, come,
And make my heart Thy happy home;
Thou wilt love me, I will love Thee,
And Thy obedient child will be.

———

**33.**

SEE, the kind Shepherd Jesus stands,
  With all engaging charms;
Hark, how He calls His tender lambs,
  And folds them in His arms.
Permit them to approach He cries,
  Nor scorn their humble name;
For 'twas to bless such souls as these
  The Lord of angels came.

He'll lead us to the heavenly streams,
  Where living waters flow,
And guide us to the fruitful fields,
  Where trees of knowledge grow.

The feeblest lamb amid the flock,
  Shall be its shepherd's care;
While folded in the Saviour's arms
  We're safe from ev'ry snare.

---

**34.**

Jesus, the water of life will give
  Freely, freely, freely,
Jesus, the water of life will give
  Freely to those who love Him.
Come to that fountain, Oh drink and live,
  Freely, freely, freely,
Come to that fountain, Oh drink and live,
  Flowing for those that love Him.

Duet:—
  The Spirit and the Bride say, come

Chorus:—Freely, freely, freely,

Duet:—
  And he that is thirsty let him come

Chorus:—
  And drink of the water of life.

Full Chorus:—
  The fountain of life is flowing,
    Flowing, freely flowing,
  The fountain of life is flowing,
    Is flowing for you and for me.

Jesus has promised a home in heaven,
  Freely, freely, freely,
Jesus has promised a home in heaven,
  Freely to those that love Him.

Treasures unfading will there be given,
    Freely, freely, freely,
Treasures unfading will there be given,
    Freely to those that love Him.
        The Spirit and the Bride, etc.


Jesus has promised a robe of white,
    Freely, freely, freely,
Jesus has promised a robe of white,
    Freely to those that love Him.
Kingdoms of glory and crowns of light,
    Freely, freely, freely,
Kingdoms of glory and crowns of light,
    Freely to those that love Him.
        The Spirit and the Bride, etc.


Jesus has promised eternal day,
    Freely, freely, freely,
Jesus has promised eternal day,
    Freely to those that love Him;
Pleasure that never shall pass away,
    Freely, freely, freely,
Pleasure that never shall pass away,
    Freely to those that love Him.
        The Spirit and the Bride, etc.


Jesus has promised a calm repose,
    Freely, freely, freely,
Jesus has promised a calm repose,
    Freely to all that love Him;

Come to the water of life that flows,
Freely, freely, freely,
Come to the water of life that flows,
Freely to all that love Him.
The Spirit and the Bride, etc.

Copyright, 1883, by Biglow & Main, used by permission.

---

**35.**

Good news for little children,
Whoever they may be,
To them the loving Saviour
Has said, "Come unto Me;"
However poor and needy,
However weak and small,
The boundless love of Jesus
Encircles one and all.

None are too young to love Him,
None are too young to know
The name of Him who saves them
From endless death and woe;
Oh, children, seek Him early,
Now in your youthful day;
He will forsake you never,
But guard you in all your ways.

Words used by arrangement with Oliver Ditson Co., owners of the copyright.

---

**36.**

Little children, come to Jesus;
Hear Him saying, "Come to Me!"
Blessed Jesus, who to save us,
Shed His blood on Calvary!

Little souls were made to serve Him,
    All His holy law fulfill;
Little hearts were made to love Him,
    Little hands to do His will.

CHORUS:—
    Little children, come to Jesus;
        Hear Him saying, "Come to Me!"
    Blessed Jesus, who to save us,
        Shed His blood on Calvary!

Little eyes to read the Bible,
    Given from the heaven above;
Little ears to hear the story
    Of the Saviour's wondrous love;
Little tongues to sing His praises,
    Little feet to walk His ways;
Little bodies to be temples
    Where the Holy Spirit, stays.

---

**37.**
I HEARD the voice of Jesus say,
    "Come unto me and rest;
Lay down, thou weary one, lay down
    Thy head upon my breast."
I came to Jesus as I was,
    Weary, and worn, and sad;
I found in Him a resting place,
    And He has made me glad.

I heard the voice of Jesus say,
    " Behold, I freely give
The living water; thirsty one,
    Stoop down and drink, and live."

I came to Jesus, and I drank
    Of that life-giving stream;
My thirst was quenched, my soul revived,
    And now I live in Him.

I heard the voice of Jesus say,
    " I am this dark world's light;
Look unto me: thy morn shall rise,
    And all thy day be bright."
I looked to Jesus, and I found
    In Him my star, my sun;
And in that light of life I'll walk
    Till traveling days are done. Amen.

Used by arrangement with S. A. Ward, owner of the copyright.

**38.**

When little Samuel woke,
    And heard his Maker's voice,
At ev'ry word He spoke,
    How much did he rejoice!
Oh, blessed, happy child! to find
The God of heaven so near and kind.

If God would speak to me,
    And say He was my friend,
How happy should I be!
    Oh, how would I attend!
The smallest sin I then should fear,
If God Almighty were so near.

And does He never speak?
    Oh, yes; for in His word,
He bids me come and seek,
    The God whom Samuel heard:
In almost ev'ry page I see,
The God of Samuel calls to me.

And I beneath His care,
  May safely rest my head,
I know that God is there,
  To guard my humble bed;
And ev'ry sin I well may fear,
Since God Almighty is so near.

Like Samuel, let me say,
  When e'er I read His word,
Speak, Lord; I would obey
  The voice that Samuel heard,
And when I in Thy house appear,
Speak, for Thy servant waits to hear.

---

**39.**

Lord, a little tired child,
  Comes to Thee this day for rest;
Take it, fold it in Thine arms,
  Soothe its head upon Thy breast;
Through a night of wind and storm,
  Lo, it leans on Thee for rest;
Take it, fold it in Thine arms,
  Soothe its head upon Thy breast.

Whisper, as it sleepeth there,
  Tenderest, sweetest lullabies,
Till it smiles as infants do,
  Dreaming of the happy skies;
Then, dear Lord, thus comforted,
  Rested with Thy perfect rest;
It shall sing to weary hearts,
  What it learned upon Thy breast.

**40.**

Tho' dark the night, and clouds look black
    And stormy overhead,
And trials of almost ev'ry kind
    Across my path are spread;
How soon I conquer all,
As to the Lord I call,
A little talk with Jesus
Makes it right, all right.

And thus by frequent little talks
    I gain the victory,
And march along with cheerful song,
    Enjoying liberty;
With Jesus as my friend
I'll prove until the end,
A little talk with Jesus
Makes it right, all right.

---

**41.**

If Jesus Christ was sent,
    To save us from our sin,
And kindly teach us to repent,
    We should at once begin.

He says He loves to see
    A broken-hearted one,
He loves that sinners such as we,
    Should mourn for what we've done.

'Tis not enough to say
    We're sorry and repent
Yet still go on from day to day
    Just as we always went.

Repentance is to leave
  The sins we loved before,
And show that we in earnest grieve
  By doing so no more.

Lord, make us thus sincere
  To watch as well as pray,
However small, however dear,
  Take all our sins away.

---

**42.**

Jesus, Thy blood and righteousness
My beauty are, my glorious dress;
'Midst flaming worlds, in these arrayed,
With joy shall I lift up my head.

Bold shall I stand in thy great day,
For who aught to my charge shall lay?
Fully absolved through these I am,
From sin and fear, from guilt and shame.

When from the dust of death I rise,
To claim my mansion in the skies,
E'en this shall then be all my plea—
Jesus hath lived, hath died, for me.

This spotless robe the same appears
When ruined nature sinks in years;
No age can change its glorious hue:
The robe of Christ is ever new.

Oh, let the dead now hear Thy voice!
Bid, Lord, Thy mourning ones rejoice:
Their beauty this, their glorious dress,
Jesus, the Lord our Righteousness.

**43.**

Rock of Ages, cleft for me,
Let me hide myself in Thee!
Let the water and the blood
From Thy wounded side that flowed
Be of sin the perfect cure,
Save from wrath, and make me pure.

Should my tears forever flow,
Should my zeal no languor know,
This for sin could not atone:
Thou must save, and Thou alone;
In my hand no price I bring,—
Simply to Thy cross I cling.

While I draw this fleeting breath,
When my eyelids close in death,
When I rise to worlds unknown;
And behold Thee on Thy throne,—
Rock of Ages, cleft for me,
Let me hide myself in Thee!

---

**44.**

I lay my sins on Jesus,
 The spotless Lamb of God;
He bears them all, and frees us
 From the accursed load.
I bring my guilt to Jesus,
 To wash my crimson stains
White in His blood most precious,
 Till not a spot remains.

I lay my wants on Jesus,
    All fullness dwells in Him;
He healeth my diseases,
    He doth my soul redeem.
I lay my griefs on Jesus,
    My burdens and my cares;
He from them all releases,
    He all my sorrows shares.

I long to be like Jesus,
    Meek, loving, lowly, mild;
I long to be like Jesus,
    The Father's holy child.
I long to be with Jesus,
    Amid the heavenly throng,
To sing with saints His praises,
    And learn the angels' song.

## 45.

THERE is a fountain filled with blood,
    Drawn from Immanuel's veins;
And sinners plunged beneath that flood,
    Lose all their guilty stains.

CHORUS:—Oh, how I love Jesus!
    Oh, how I love Jesus!
    Oh, how I love Jesus,
        Because He first loved me.

The dying thief rejoiced to see
    That fountain in his day;
And there may I, as vile as he,
    Wash all my sins away.

Dear dying Lamb, Thy precious blood
   Shall never lose its power
Till all the ransomed church of God
   Be saved, to sin no more.

E'er since by faith, I saw the stream
   Thy flowing wounds supply,
Redeeming love has been my theme,
   And shall be till I die.

Then in a nobler, sweeter song,
   I'll sing Thy power to save,
When this poor lisping, stammering tongue
   Lies silent in the grave.

---

**46.**

According to Thy gracious word,
   In meek humility,
This will I do, my dying Lord,—
   I will remember Thee!

Can I Gethsemane forget,
   Or there Thy conflict see,
Thine agony and bloody sweat,
   And not remember Thee?

When to the Cross I turn mine eyes,
   And rest on Calvary,
O Lamb of God! my Sacrifice!
   I must remember Thee.

Remember Thee, and all Thy pains,
   And all Thy love to me!
Yes, while a breath, a pulse remains,
   I will remember Thee!

And when these failing lips grow dumb,
And mind and memory flee,
When Thou shalt in Thy kingdom come,
Jesus! remember me.

---

**47.**

My faith looks up to Thee,
Thou Lamb of Calvary,
　Saviour divine:
Now hear me while I pray,
Take all my guilt away;
Oh let me from this day
　Be wholly thine.

May Thy rich grace impart
Strength to my fainting heart,
　My zeal inspire:
As thou hast died for me,
Oh may my love to Thee
Pure, warm and changeless be,
　A living fire.

While life's dark maze I tread,
And griefs around me spread,
　Be Thou my Guide;
Bid darkness turn to day,
Wipe sorrow's tears away,
Nor let me ever stray
　From Thee aside.

When ends life's transient dream,
When death's cold, sullen stream
　Shall o'er me roll,
Blest Saviour, then in love,
Fear and distrust remove;
Oh bear me safe above,
　A ransomed soul.

**48.**

    Just as I *am* without one plea
    But that Thy *blood* was shed for me,
    And that Thou *bid'st* me come to Thee,
        O *Lamb* of God, I come!

    Just as I am, and waiting not
    To rid my soul of one dark blot,
    To Thee, whose blood can cleanse each spot,
        O Lamb of God, I come!

    Just as I am, though tossed about
    With many a conflict, many a doubt,
    Fightings within, and fears without,
        O Lamb of God, I come!

    Just as I am, poor, wretched, blind;
    Sight, riches, healing of the mind,
    Yea, all I need, in Thee to find,
        O Lamb of God, I come!

    Just as I am, Thou wilt receive,
    Wilt welcome, pardon, cleanse, relieve;
    Because Thy promise I believe,
        O Lamb of God, I come!

    Just as I am—Thy love unknown
    Has broken every barrier down—
    Now, to be Thine, yea, Thine alone,
        O Lamb of God, I come! Amen.

**49.**

I WANT to be like Jesus,
   So lowly and so meek,
For no one marked an angry word
   That ever heard Him speak;
I want to be like Jesus,
   So frequently in prayer,
Alone upon the mountain top,
   He met His Father there.

I want to be like Jesus,
   I never, never find
That He though persecuted was
   To any one unkind;
I want to be like Jesus,
   Engaged in doing good,
So that of me it may be said,
   She hath done what she could.

I want to be like Jesus,
   So lowly and so meek,
For no one marked an angry word
   That ever heard Him speak;
Alas! I'm not like Jesus
   As any one may see,
O gentle Saviour, send Thy grace,
   And make me like to Thee.

---

**50.**

JESUS, when a little child
   Taught us what we ought to be—
Holy, harmless, undefiled
   Was the Saviour's infancy;
All the Father's glory shone
In the person of His Son.

As in age and strength He grew,
    Heavenly wisdom filled His breast;
Crowds attentive, round Him drew,
    Wondering at their infant guest;
Gazed upon His lovely face,
Saw Him full of truth and grace.

In His heavenly Father's house
    Jesus spent His early days;
There He paid His solemn vows,
    There proclaimed His Father's praise,
Thus it was His lot to gain,
Favor both with God and man.

Father, guide our steps aright
    In the way that Jesus trod;
May it be our great delight
    To obey Thy will, O God!
Then to us shall soon be given
Endless bliss with Christ in heaven.

---

**51.**

The Author of salvation,
    The Saviour, meek and mild;
Once took a lowly station,
    Became a little child.
In infancy, a stranger,
    How mean was His abode!
His cradle was a manger,
    Himself the Son of God.

Cho.—The Author of salvation,
    The Saviour, meek and mild;
Once took a lowly station,
    Became a little child.

His earthly parents found Him,
    Submissive, day by day;
So meek to all around Him,
    So ready to obey.
No stain of sin or folly,
    Could ever cloud His brow;
His heart, so pure and holy,
    With love would ever glow.

And when His foes assailed Him,
    He sought but to forgive;
When to the cross they nailed Him,
    He died that they might live.
This bright example shows us,
    What duties to fulfill;
Oh, let it now arouse us,
    To hear and do His will.

---

**52.**

THE foxes have their dwelling,
    The little birds their nest,
But God's own Son, that blessed One,
    Had not a place for rest;
A lonely mountain pillow
    His sleeping place might be,
And kneeling there in nightly prayer
    His own remembered He.

A thousand tongues are calling
    This loyal heart of mine,
And gilded toys and fleeting joys
    Around my pathway shine;
But, oh, they seem as nothing
    Since Christ my heart has won;
I'll walk His ways and sing His praise
    Till traveling days are done.

**53.**

Whene'er my angry passions rise,
    And tempt my heart and tongue to strife,
To Jesus let me lift mine eyes,
    Bright pattern of the Christian's life.

Oh, how benevolent and kind,
    How mild and ready to forgive;
Be this the temper of our mind,
    And these the rules by which we live.

To do His Heavenly Father's will
    Was His employment and delight;
Humility and holy zeal,
    Shone through His life supremely bright.

But oh, how blind, how weak we are,
    How frail, how apt to turn aside!
Lord, we depend upon Thy care,
    We ask Thy Spirit for our guide.

Thy fair example may we trace
    To teach us what we ought to be;
Make us by Thy transforming grace,
    O Saviour, daily more like Thee.

---

**54.**

More like Jesus would I be,
Let my Saviour dwell in me;
Fill my soul with peace and love,
Make me gentle as the dove.

More like Jesus while I go,
Pilgrim in this world below;
Poor in spirit would I be,
Let my Saviour dwell in me.

If He hears the raven's cry,
If His ever watchful eye,
Marks the sparrows when they fall,
Surely He will hear my call.

He will teach me how to live,
All my sinful thoughts forgive;
Pure in heart, I still would be—
Let my Saviour dwell in me.

---

**55.**

This day belongs to God alone
This day He chooses for His own,
And we must neither work nor play,
Because it is God's holy day.
'Tis well to have one day in seven,
That we may learn the way to heaven,
Then let us spend it as we should,
In serving God and being good.

We ought to-day to learn and seek,
What we may think of all the week,
And be the better ev'ry day,
For what we hear our teachers say.
Then let us ever watch and pray,
And holy keep the Sabbath day,
That we may Jesus learn to love,
And dwell with Him in heaven above.

**56.**

We must not work on Sunday,
On Sunday, on Sunday,
We must not work on Sunday,
  Because it is a sin.
But we may work on Monday,
On Tuesday, on Wednesday,
On Thursday, Friday, Saturday,
  'Till Sunday comes again.

We must not play on Sunday,
On Sunday, on Sunday,
We must not play on Sunday,
  Because it is a sin.
But we may play on Monday,
On Tuesday, on Wednesday,
On Thursday, Friday, Saturday,
  'Till Sunday comes again.

We must not buy on Sunday,
On Sunday, on Sunday,
We must not buy on Sunday,
  Because it is a sin.
But we may buy on Monday,
On Tuesday, on Wednesday,
On Thursday, Friday, Saturday,
  'Till Sunday comes again.

We must not sell on Sunday,
On Sunday, on Sunday,
We must not sell on Sunday,
  Because it is a sin.
But we may sell on Monday,
On Tuesday, on Wednesday,
On Thursday, Friday, Saturday
  'Till Sunday comes again.

We must do wrong on no day,
On no day, on no day,
We must do wrong on no day,
  Because it is a sin.
But serve the Lord on Monday,
On Tuesday, on Wednesday,
On Thursday, Friday, Saturday,
  'Till Sunday comes again.

---

**57.**

Ring, Sabbath bells, ring merrily
  And fill our hearts with praise,
Ring on, we'll sing so cheerily
  To God, our thoughts we'll raise;
From far and near, from everywhere
  Bring little children home,
Into this happy house of God,
  'Tis Jesus bids them come.

Ring, joyful bells, ring merrily,
  And sound your loudest chime,
Ring out your music joyfully
  In sweet and tuneful rhyme;
For though our Christ was humbly born
  And in a manger lay,
Yet He is God, the King of kings
  To whom we all should pray.

Ring, Sabbath bells, ring merrily,
  While childish voices swell,
In this our song of loving praise
  To Christ we love so well;
Upon the cross He gave His life
  That we might be forgiven,
He shows us all the pathway bright
  That leads from earth to heaven.

**58.**

How sweet is the Sabbath, the morning of rest;
The day of the week which I surely love best;
The morning my Saviour arose from the tomb,
And took from the grave all its terror and gloom.

Oh let me be thoughtful and prayerful to-day,
And not spend a minute in trifling or play;
Remembering these seasons were graciously given,
To teach me to seek, and prepare me for heaven.

In the house of my God, in His presence and fear;
When I worship to-day may it all be sincere;
In the school when I learn, may I do it with care,
And be grateful to those who watch over me there.

Instruct me, my Saviour, a child though I be;
I am not too young to be noticed by Thee;
Renew all my heart, keep me firm in Thy ways,
I would love Thee and serve Thee, and give Thee
    the praise.

---

(*Recite.*)    FIRST COMMANDMENT.

Thou shalt have no other gods before me.

## SECOND COMMANDMENT.

Thou shalt not make unto thee any graven image, or any likeness *of any thing* that *is* in heaven above, or that *is* in the earth beneath, or that *is* in the water under the earth: thou shalt not bow down thyself to them, nor serve them: for I the Lord thy God *am* a jealous God, visiting the iniquity of the fathers upon the children unto the third and fourth *generation* of them that hate me; and shewing mercy unto thousands of them that love me, and keep my commandments.

### THIRD COMMANDMENT.

Thou shalt not take the name of the Lord thy God in vain: for the Lord will not hold him guiltless that taketh his name in vain.
(*Sing.*)

**59.      Commandment Hymn.**

One God I must worship supreme,
  And ne'er before images bow;
I must not speak light of His name,
  But pay to Him every vow.


I'm bound to remember with care
  The Sabbath so hallowed and pure;
To honor my parents so dear,
  That my life may the longer endure.


I never must steal, nor consent
  To what is impure or untrue;
I must not indulge discontent,
  Or covet my neighbor his due.


Now help me, O Father in heaven,
  To keep these commandments with zeal,
In the strength that through Jesus is given,
  To those who are doing Thy will.

## (*Recite.*) FOURTH COMMANDMENT.

Remember the Sabbath day, to keep it holy. Six days shalt thou labour, and do all thy work: but the seventh day *is* the Sabbath of the Lord thy God: *in it* thou shalt not do any work, thou, nor thy son, nor thy daughter, thy manservant, nor thy maidservant, nor thy cattle, nor thy stranger that *is* within thy gates: for *in* six days the Lord made heaven and earth, the sea, and all that in them *is*, and rested the seventh day: wherefore the Lord blessed the Sabbath day, and hallowed it.

## FIFTH COMMANDMENT.

Honor thy father and thy mother: that thy days may be long upon the land which the Lord thy God giveth thee.

(*Sing.*) I'm bound to remember with care,
    The Sabbath so hallowed and pure;
  To honor my parents so dear,
    That my life may the longer endure.

## (*Recite.*) SIXTH COMMANDMENT.

Thou shalt not kill.

## SEVENTH COMMANDMENT.

Thou shalt not commit adultery.

## EIGHTH COMMANDMENT.

Thou shalt not steal.

## NINTH COMMANDMENT.

Thou shalt not bear false witness against thy neighbor.

## TENTH COMMANDMENT.

Thou shalt not covet thy neighbour's house, thou shalt not covet thy neighbour's wife, nor his manservant, nor his maidservant, nor his ox, nor his ass, nor anything that *is* thy neighbour's.

(*Sing.*)
>I never must steal, nor consent,
>  To what is impure or untrue;
>I must not indulge discontent,
>  Or covet my neighbor his due.

(*Recite.*)

### THE TWO GREAT COMMANDMENTS.

Thou shalt love the Lord thy God with all thy heart, and with all thy soul, and with all thy mind, and with all thy strength: this *is* the first commandment. And the second *is* like, *namely* this, Thou shalt love thy neighbour as thyself.—MARK 12: 30, 31.

(*Sing.*)
>Now help me, O Father in heaven,
>  To keep these commandments with zeal,
>In the strength that through Jesus is given,
>  To those who are doing Thy will.

---

**60.**

>From sinful words I must refrain;
>I must not take God's name in vain
>I must not work, I must not play,
>Upon God's holy Sabbath day.

>And if my parents speak the word,
>I must obey them in the Lord;
>Nor steal, nor lie, nor waste my days
>In idle tales and foolish plays.

**61.**
 The deadly cup while others drink,
  We'll never, never taste it;
 It lures us on to ruin's brink,
  And thousands have confessed it;
 Come, boys and girls, the pledge we'll sign,
  Be temperance sons and daughters;
 We'll banish brandy, rum, and wine,
  And drink the crystal waters.

 We'll never take God's name in vain,
  And never will profane it;
 The virtuous heart shall ne'er complain
  Our oaths alarm and pain it;
 No words profane our lips shall move,
  No words untrue defile them;
 And swearers we'll entreat in love,
  And pray for, not revile them.

 We'll never use the filthy weed
  We taste at first with loathing,
 Which pales the cheek all blooming red,
  And scents the breath and clothing:
 If we beneath its power should fall,
  'Twill prove a cruel master,
 Around us throws its iron thrall
  And bind the captive faster.

 Then come, a war we'll nobly wage
  With all that would degrade us;
 The foe may meet us in his rage,
  But God will surely aid us:
 No tyrant habit e'er shall sit
  Enthroned and crowned within us;
 True life these things but ill befit,
  'Tis love divine shall win us.

**62.**

    Of all the tints the light looks on,
        However bright their hue,
    There's none that speaks of better things
        Than does the bit of blue.

Refrain :—
    The bonnie bit of blue, my friends,
        The bonnie bit of blue.
    It tells of hope, it tells of joy,
        The bonnie bit of blue.

    Come, wear the blue—you cannot know
        The good that you may do,
    By joining in a noble cause,
        The Army of the blue.

    Then wear the blue above the heart
        That's brave, and warm and true,
    And never be ashamed to show
        The bonnie bit of blue.

---

**63.**

### A Recitation.

There is a boy (perhaps you know his name)—
Who tried to shun the way that leads to shame :
The way that tipplers go, and drunkards love,
The way uncheered by blessing from above.
From jacket front a ribbon blue depends,
To show that he and *Temperance* are good friends.
It is a *badge*, more worthy to be worn
Than many emblems that a prince adorn.
A generous leader—Temperance takes great care
Of all her followers—precious gifts they share :

*Health, happy homes*, and *self-respect;* how true
*Their wealth*, who wear the "*Bonnie bit of Blue.*"
The "Bonnie bit of Blue" long may it wave,
Our girls and boys from Demon Drink to save!
Do you not wear it? Then begin to now,
With which advice, I close, and make my bow.
      Song. Bonnie bit of blue.
        [Children waving blue streamers.]

---

## 64.

IN the ways of true temperance see children delight-
    ing,
  So joyful and happy wherever we go;
If firm to the purpose in which we're uniting,
  We shall never be drunkards, Oh, never, oh, no!

CHORUS:—

  Oh, never, oh, never, oh, never, oh, never,
  We shall never be drunkards, oh, never, oh, no!

The first little drop of strong drink that is taken,
  Is the first step to ruin, e'en children may know;
If the first little drop be in earnest forsaken,
  We shall never be drunkards, Oh, never, oh, no!

Then free from the ruin strong drink would occa-
    sion,
  We'll stand by our temperance wherever we go,
If evil ones tempt, we'll resist their persuasion,
  And never be drunkards, Oh, never, oh, no!

From Gathered Jewels No. 2, by per. of W. W. Whitney Co.

**65.**

Come children come, join the Temperance band,
    Now in your day of youth,
Dark hang the clouds o'er our native land,
    Come fight for right and truth.
Many the children, weeping to-day,
    Sorrowing for loved ones now gone,
Slain by the cruel tyrant Rum,
    Leaving their sad ones to mourn.

REFRAIN :—
    Come children come, join the Temperance fight,
        Bright gleams our banner to-day,
    Be not dismayed we are marching in might,
        Soon will the mist roll away.

Children are gathering over the land,
    Gathering to help fight the foe,
Satan is arming his mighty band,
    To bring our nation low.
Then, oh, dear children, drive Rum away,
    And if you have touched it before,
Let not the Tempter, lead you astray,
    But watch and pray evermore.

---

**66.**

Don't drink it, boys, don't drink it
    Put the tempting glass away;
'Twill surely be your ruin, boys;
    Remember what I say;
Now promise from this moment, boys,
    You'll never drink again:
Come out in God's own sunshine, boys,
    And sign the pledge like men.

Don't drink it, boys, don't drink it;
  It's the source of every crime;
It biteth like a serpent, boys;
  Beware! be warned in time:
Perchance the voice that warns you now,
  You'll never hear again;
Come out in God's own sunlight, boys,
  And sign the pledge like men.

Don't drink it, boys, don't drink it;
  You will rue it if you do;
Oh! think how many loving hearts
  Are praying now for you:
Now promise in the fear of God,
  You'll never drink again;
Come, join the temperance army, boys,
  And sign the pledge like men.

Copyright, 1874, by Hubert P. Main. Used by per.

---

**67.**

Mourn for the thousands slain,
  The youthful and the strong;
Mourn for the wine-cup's fearful reign,
  And the deluded throng.

Mourn for the ruined soul—
  Eternal life and light
Lost by the fiery, maddening bowl,
  And turned to hopeless night.

Mourn for the lost—but call,
  Call to the strong, the free;
Rouse them to shun that dreadful fall,
  And to the refuge flee.

Mourn for the lost—but pray,
  Pray to our God above,
To break the fell destroyer's sway,
  And show His saving love.

---

## 68.

"Wine is a mocker, strong drink is raging: and whosoever is deceived thereby is not wise."—PROV. 20: 1.

A PLEDGE we make
No wine to take;
Nor brandy red,
To turn the head;
Nor whiskey hot,
That makes the sot;
Nor fiery rum,
That ruins home.
Nor will we sin,
By drinking gin;
Hard cider, too,
Will never do;
Nor brewer's beer,
Our hearts to cheer.
To quench our thirst, we always bring
Cold water, from the well or spring;
So here we pledge perpetual hate
To all that can intoxicate.

**69.**

Away from the dusty highway,
    Afar from the crowded street,
There sparkled a cooling fountain,
    Which murmured in music sweet,

DUETT.—Its melody so enchanting,
    As through the air it rung,
Methought as I staid to listen,
    That these were the words it sung:

CHO.—O come ye and drink of the nectar
    Which health and prosperity brings,
For the foam of the sparkling wine-cup,
    At last like an adder it stings.

Though death and destruction lieth
    Concealed in the drunkard's bowl,
Yet thousands have lost their manhood,
    And bartered away the soul,

DUETT.—For a drink of the fiery cordial
    Which leads to the drunkard's grave,
Which maketh the man a demon,
    And maketh the king a slave.

Oh, turn from the path of evil,
    That seemeth so fair and broad,
For, surely, no drunkard ever,
    Can enter the kingdom of God,

DUETT.—We'll drink of thy water, sweet fountain,
    Till, free from contention and strife,
We'll dwell in the beautiful Eden,
    And drink of the river of life.

**70.**

Come all ye little children,
   And heaken unto me;
While now I teach you all the way,
   To find true liberty.

Cho.—Children! Children!
Won't you join the band of Temp'rance, Temp'rance,
   Marching through the land!

With beer, and ale and cider,
   We'll nothing have to do;
Or brandy, or rum, or whisky,
   And neither too should you.

If you wish to be happy
   At home and full of cheer;
You must banish all the brandy,
   And wine, and gin, and beer.

For those who early learn to drink,
   Can never happy be;
But walk the way that leads to death,
   And endless misery.

To touch not, taste not, handle not,
   Must ever be our rule;
And this we all are learning,
   In our dear Sabbath-school.

And God who lives in heaven,
  Is ever pleased to see;
Our efforts to lead others,
  To walk in wisdom's way.

Copyright, 1896, by E. Revere.

NOTE.—Gather the children around the platform who are about to take the pledge. Have them repeat the pledge in concert, then pin a badge upon each child's bosom. Sing the Temperance Hymn. Explain the pledge, and march the children to sign their names in the book. Give also each child a card pledge to keep.

---

## 71.

TOUCH not the cup it is death to thy soul,
  Touch not the cup, touch not the cup,
Many I know who have quaffed from that bowl,
  Touch not the cup, touch it not.
Little they thought that the demon was there
Blindly they drank and were caught in the snare,
Then of that death dealing bowl, oh beware;
  Touch not the cup, touch it not.

Touch not the cup when the wine glistens bright,
  Touch not the cup, touch not the cup,
Though like the ruby it shines in the light,
  Touch not the cup, touch it not.
Fangs of the serpent, are hid in the bowl,
Deeply the poison may enter thy soul,
Soon will it plunge thee beyond thy control,
  Touch not the cup, touch it not.

'Touch not the cup, oh, do not drink a drop,
  Touch not the cup, touch not the cup,
All that thou lovest entreat thee to stop,
  Touch not the cup, touch it not.
Stop! for the home that to thee is so dear,
Stop! for the friends that to thee, are so near,
Stop! for thy country in trembling and fear,
  Touch not the cup, touch it not.

---

## 72.

We are coming, we are coming,
  Make us room throughout the land;
Children strong, and happy children,
  Who have joined the Temperance Band.
We have promised not to handle,
  Touch or taste the cup of woe;
We will fight with God against it,
  This our country's deadliest foe.

If our fathers and our mothers
  Drink, they know not what they do;
We are taught a better lesson,
  And we'll heed it brave and true.
If we never learn to love it,
  Grown to women and to men;
Older, stronger, nobler, purer,
  We shall never want it then.

---

## 73.

I promise Thee, sweet Lord, that I
  Will never cloud the light
Which shines from Thee within my soul,
  And makes my reason bright;

Nor ever will I lose the power
    To serve Thee by my will,
Which Thou hast set within my heart,
    Thy precepts to fulfill.


Oh, let me drink as Adam drank,
    Before from Thee he fell,
Oh, let me drink as Thou, dear Lord,
    When faint by Sychar's well,
That from my childhood, pure from sin
    Of drink and drunken strife,
By the clear fountains, I may rest,
    Of everlasting life.

---

**74.**

Do unto others what we would expect,
They should do unto us, never neglect
Each other's grief to share, and we shall gain
Kindness and pity when we are in pain.


Let all our actions be guided by love,
This is the law of God, sent from above,
And if we daily try, with all our might,
We with His help can do, just what is right.


Jesus our loving Lord gave us this text,
Love first thy God in heav'n, thy neighbor next,
So shall earth's kingdom be like that above,
Love is the law of God, for God is love.

**75.**

Little children love each other,
  Is the blessed Saviour's rule,
Ev'ry little one is brother,
  To his mates in Sabbath-school.
We're all children of one Father,
  The great God who lives above,
Shall we quarrel? no, much rather,
  We would be like Him, all love.

Selfish children's bad behavior,
  Shows they love themselves alone,
But the children of the Saviour,
  Say not anything is their own.
All they have, they share with others,
  Give kind looks and gentle words,
Thus they live like happy brothers,
  And are known to be the Lord's.

---

**76.**

To do to others as I would
  That they should do to me,
Will make me honest, kind and good,
  As children ought to be.
I know I should not steal nor use
  The smallest thing I see,
Which I should never like to lose
  If it belonged to me.

And this plain rule forbids me quite
  To strike an angry blow,
Because I should not think it right
  If others served me so.
But any kindness they may need
  I'll do, whate'er it be;
As I am very glad indeed
  When they are kind to me.

**77.**

    Oh, the sweet, sweet words of Jesus,
        Silver, silver bells!
    Listen, children, for their music
        Wondrous tidings tells;
    How to make this world of ours
        Blossom as the rose;
    How a child may carry sunshine
        Wheresoe'er it goes.

    "Little children, love each other,"
        This is one sweet chime;
    Then a little longer message
        Comes another time.
    Do you know it? "Do to others
        As ye would that they
    Should do unto you," comes sounding
        Through your work and play.

    Let the sweet, sweet bells of Jesus
        Ring through all your life;
    They shall soothe its ev'ry trouble,
        Calm its ev'ry strife.
    Oh, the sweet, sweet words of Jesus,
        Silver, silver bells!
    Listen, children, for their music
        Wondrous tidings tells.

---

**78.**
Our Heav'nly King, from His throne above,
Sends down to us His law of Love,
A silken cord our hearts to bind,
In brotherhood with all mankind.

A silken cord our hearts to raise,
To Him who merits all our praise,
A silken cord our hearts to raise,
To Him who merits all our praise.

Our Heav'nly King, from His throne above,
Sends down to us His law of Love,
Like perfume from the fragrant flow'r,
Will be our lives beneath its power.
Yes, like the fragrant flow'rs perfume,
That gladdens all within its room,
Yes, like the fragrant flow'rs perfume,
That gladdens all within its room.

Our Heav'nly King, from His throne above,
Sends down to us His law of Love:
A royal law from the King's own hand,
A message kind from Fatherland.
The King's own children day by day,
Best honor Him, who best obey,
The King's own children day by day,
Best honor Him, who best obey.

---

## 79.

God so loved the world, that he gave his only begotten Son, that whosoever believeth in him should not perish, but have everlasting life.—John 3 : 16.

A new commandment I give unto you, That ye love one another.—John 13 : 34.

My little children, let us not love in word, neither in tongue; but in deed and in truth.
—1 John 3 : 18.

## LOVE.

1. Charity suffereth long and is kind;—
2. Charity envieth not.
3. Charity vaunteth not itself, is not puffed up.
4. Doth not behave itself unseemly.
5. Seeketh not her own.
6. Is not easily provoked.
7. Thinketh no evil.
8. Rejoiceth not in inquity, but rejoiceth in the truth.
9. Beareth all things.
10. Believeth all things.
11. Hopeth all things, endureth all things.
12. Charity never faileth.—1 COR. 13 : 4-8.

Now abideth faith, hope, charity, these three; but the greatest of these *is* charity.—1 COR. 13 : 13.

Reprinted by per. from " The Pansy."

---

**80.**

There is beauty all around,
　When there's love at home;
There is joy in ev'ry sound,
　When there's love at home.
Peace and plenty here abide,
Smiling sweet on ev'ry side;
Time doth softly, sweetly glide,
　When there's love at home,
Love at home, Love at home,
Time doth softly, sweetly glide,
　When there's love at home.

In the cottage there is joy,
   When there's love at home;
Hate and envy ne'er annoy,
   When there's love at home.
Roses blossom 'neath our feet,
All the earth's a garden sweet,
Making life a bliss complete,
   When there's love at home,
Love at home, Love at home,
Making life a bliss complete,
   When there's love at home.

Kindly heaven smiles above,
   When there's love at home;
All the earth is filled with love,
   When there's love at home.
Sweeter sings the brooklet by,
Brighter beams the azure sky:
Oh, there's One who smiles on high,
   When there's love at home,
   Love at home, Love at home,
Oh, there's One who smiles on high,
   When there's love at home.

Jesus, show Thy mercy mine,
   Then there's love at home;
Sweetly whisper I am Thine,
   Then there's love at home.
Source of love, Thy cheering light
Far exceeds the sun so bright—
Can dispel the gloom of night;
   Then there's love at home,
   Love at home, Love at home,
Can dispel the gloom of night,
   Then there's love at home.

**Used by per. of O. Ditson Co., owners of copyright.**

**81.**

Words are things of little cost,
Quickly spoken, quickly lost;
We forget them; but they stand
Witnesses at God's right hand,
And their testimonies bear,
For us or against us there.

Oh, how often ours have been
Idle words and words of sin,
Words of anger, scorn, or pride,
Or deceit, or faults to hide,
Envious tales, or strife unkind,
Leaving bitter thoughts behind!

Grant us, Lord, from day to day,
Strength to watch and grace to pray;
May our lips, from sin kept free,
Love to speak and sing of Thee—
Till in heav'n we learn to raise
Hymns of everlasting praise.

---

**82.**

One step and then another,
   And the longest walk is ended;
One stitch and then another,
   And the largest rent is mended.
One brick upon another,
   And the highest wall is made.
One flake upon another,
   And the deepest snow is laid.

Then do not look disheartened
  On the work you have to do,
And say that such a mighty task
  You never can get through.
But just endeavor day by day,
  Another point to gain,
And soon the mountain which you fear
  Will prove to be a plain.

Rome was not builded in a day,
  The ancient proverb teaches;
And nature by her trees and flowers,
  The same sweet lesson preaches.
Think not of far-off duties,
  But of duties which are near,
And having once begun to work,
  Resolve to persevere.

---

**83.**

Here's a lesson all should heed,
  Try again, try again;
If at first you don't succeed,
  Try, oh, try again.
Let your courage well appear,
  Only persevere,
You will conquer, never fear,
  Try, oh, try again.

Chorus.—Here's a lesson all should heed,
  Try again, try again;
If at first you don't succeed,
  Try, oh, try again.

Twice or thrice, tho' you should fail,
    Try again, try again;
If at last you would prevail,
    Try, oh, try again.
When you strive there's no disgrace,
    Though you fail to win,
Bravely then in such a case,
    Try, oh, try again.

Let the thing be e'er so hard,
    Try again, try again;
Time will surely bring reward,
    Try, oh, try again.
That which other folks can do,
    Why may not you?
Why with patience may not you?
    Try, oh, try again.

---

**84.**

Never be afraid to speak for Jesus,
    Think how much a word can do;
Never be afraid to own your Saviour,
    He, who loves and cares for you.

Cho.—Never be afraid, never be afraid,
    Never, never, never,
  Jesus is your loving Saviour,
    Therefore never be afraid.

Never be afraid to work for Jesus,
    In His vineyard day by day;
Labor with a kind and willing spirit,
    He will all your toil repay.

Never be afraid to bear for Jesus,
  Keen reproaches when they fall;
Patiently endure your ev'ry trial,
  Jesus meekly bore them all.

Copyright, 1883, Biglow & Main, used by permission.

**85.**
I was but a little lamb
  From the Shepherd straying,
When I heard within my heart
  Some One softly saying:—

Chorus:—" Follow Me, follow Me,
    I will safely guide thee
  Through the stormy ways of life,
    Walking with thee."

Into danger I would go
  But for His protection;
I should miss of heaven, I know,
  But for this direction:—

Never turning from that voice,
  Never disobeying,
Let me know that unto me
  Christ is always saying:—

Early to His loving care
  Shall my heart be given,
For each step I take with Him
  Brings me nearer heaven.

*Chorus for last verse.*
  "Follow Me, follow Me,"
    Is the Saviour saying
  Unto ev'ry little lamb
    Straying away.

**86.**

Whene'er you see a schoolboy
   Who climbs the orchard fence,
Or sneaks around the corner
   To steal the apple and quince.

Refrain:—
   Tell him to halt! tell him to halt!
   Whatever may be his fault.
   Tell him to halt! tell him to halt!
   Whatever may be his fault;
   Play up the little Captain,
   The brave and gallant Captain,
   And tell him to halt!
   Halt! halt! halt!

Whene'er you see him loafing,
   Who ought to be at school,
Or playing the idle truant
   Against the teacher's rule.

Whene'er you see him fighting,
   Or brawling in the street,
Or playing the schoolboy bully,
   The meanest thing you meet.

Whene'er you hear him swearing,
   Or saying the naughty word,
Or telling a lie or tattling
   Of something he has heard.

Don't let the devil lead him
   In ways of burning shame,
Speak up, ye gallant Captain,
   And call him by his name.

But when you see him doing
   The thing he ought to do,
And when you hear him speaking,
   The word so good and true.

*For last stanza.*

Tell him to march! tell him to march!
Right under the Christian arch.
Tell him to march! tell him to march!
Right under the Christian arch;
Play up the little Captain,
The brave and gallant Captain,
And tell him to march!
March! march! march!

**Used by permission of Dr. H. R. Palmer, owner of copyright.**

---

**87.**

My soul, be on thy guard;
   Ten thousand foes arise,
And hosts of sin are pressing hard
   To draw thee from the skies.

Oh, watch and fight and pray,
   The battle ne'er give o'er;
Renew it boldly ev'ry day,
   And help divine implore.

Ne'er think the victory won,
   Nor once at ease sit down;
Thine arduous work will not be done
   Till thou hast got thy crown.

**88.**

    YIELD not to temptation,
      For yielding is sin,
    Each victory will help you
      Some other to win;
    Fight manfully onward,
      Dark passion subdue,
    Look ever to Jesus,
      He'll carry you through.

CHORUS.—Ask the Saviour to help you,
        Comfort, strengthen, and keep you;
    He is willing to aid you,
      He will carry you through.

    Shun evil companions,
      Bad language disdain,
    God's name hold in reverence,
      Nor take it in vain;
    Be thoughtful and earnest,
      Kind hearted and true,
    Look ever to Jesus,
      He'll carry you through.

    To him that o'ercometh
      God giveth a crown,
    Through faith we shall conquer,
      Though often cast down;
    He who is our Saviour,
      Our strength will renew,
    Look ever to Jesus,
      He'll carry you through.

Used by permission of Dr. H. R. Palmer, owner of copyright.

**89.**

As the soft, departing rays
   Of the sun fade in the west,
Hear, O Lord, our hymn of praise,
   For this holy day of rest.

Through our lives may we retain
   The blest lessons we have heard,
And in sorrow, sin or pain,
   Teach us to turn to Thy Word.

When our journey here is o'er,
   May our souls in heaven awake,
Safely on the shining shore,
   And all we ask for Jesus' sake.   Amen.

---

**90.**

SOFTLY whisper, softly speak,
Little children, still and meek;
Hush and listen, do not play,
Hear what Teacher has to say.

When we sing, and when we pray,
When from sin we turn away;
When our hearts to Jesus rise,
Jesus answers from the skies.

Father, Spirit, now would we
With our spirits worship Thee;
Thine own Spirit may we share,
Love and serve Thee everywhere.

**91.**

**1.**

I BELIEVE in God the Father
(Raise the right hand.)
Who made the Heaven and earth,
(Both hands raised and then pointing down.)
The sea, and all that is therein;
(Moving the hands like water.)
In Him we have our birth.
(Cross hands on the breast.)
The Sun, and Moon, the Stars and sky
(Raise hands and twinkle with fingers.)
Were made by Him above,
In prayer we lift our hearts to Him
(Place the hands together as in prayer, and look up.)
And trust in His great love.

**2.**

I believe in Christ the Saviour,
(Raise both hands.)
The blessed Son of God;
Who came on earth to save us,
(Lower the hands slowly.)
And shed His precious blood.
To take from us all sin and woe,
Upon the cross He died,
(Raise both hands palms out, as though nailed to cross.)
That all our sins might be forgiven,
(Hand on heart.)
Our Lord was crucified.

**3.**

I believe in God the Spirit,
(Raise the hand, pointing up.)
Sent to us from on high,
Who by His grace, renews our hearts
(Hand on the heart.)

And hears our humble cry.
Dear Father! help us day by day
(Hands together as in prayer.)
To grow in faith and love,
That we at last may dwell with Thee
In Thy blest home above.
(Look up and raise hands to Heaven.)
Copyright, 1896, by E. Revere.

---

**92.**

Saviour! when in dust to Thee
Low we bow th' adoring knee;
When, repentant, to the skies
Scarce we lift our streaming eyes,—
Oh! by all Thy pain and woe,
Suffered once for man below,
Bending from Thy throne on high,
Hear our solemn litany.

By Thy birth and early years,
By Thy human griefs and fears,
By Thy fasting and distress
In the lonely wilderness,
By Thy victory in the hour
Of the subtle tempter's power,—
Jesus! look with pitying eye;
Hear our solemn litany.

By Thy conflict with despair,
By Thine agony of prayer,
By Thy purple robe of scorn,
By Thy wounds, Thy crown of thorn,
By Thy cross, Thy pangs and cries,
By Thy perfect sacrifice,—
Jesus! look with pitying eye;
Hear our solemn litany.

**93.**

Now I lay me down to sleep,
I pray Thee, Lord, my soul to keep;
If I should die before I wake,
I pray Thee, Lord, my soul to take.

---

**94.**

Jesus, Saviour, pity me,
Hear me when I cry to Thee;
I've a very wicked heart,
Full of sin in ev'ry part.

I can never make it good;
Wilt Thou wash me in Thy blood?
Jesus, Saviour, pity me,
Hear me when I pray to Thee.

When I try to do Thy will,
Sin is in my bosom still,
And I soon do something bad;
Then my heart is dark and sad.

Now I come to Thee for aid,
All my hope on Thee is stayed;
Thou hast bled and died for me,
I will give myself to Thee.

---

**95.**

When daily I kneel down to pray,
   As I am taught to do,
God does not care for what I say,
   Unless I feel it, too.

Yet foolish thoughts my heart beguile,
    And when I pray or sing,
I'm often thinking all the while
    About some other thing.

Oh, let me never, never dare
    To act a trifler's part,
Or think that God will hear a prayer
    That comes not from the heart.

But if I make His ways my choice,
    As holy children do,
Then while I seek Him with my voice,
    My heart will love Him too.

## 96.

Lord Jesus, I long to be perfectly whole;
I want Thee for ever to live in my soul;
Break down ev'ry idol, cast out ev'ry foe;
Now wash me, and I shall be whiter than snow.

Chorus:
    Whiter than snow, yes, whiter than snow;
    Now wash me, and I shall be whiter than snow.

Lord Jesus, look down from Thy throne in the skies,
And help me to make a complete sacrifice;
I give up myself, and whatever I know;
Now wash me, and I shall be whiter than snow.

Dear Jesus, for this I most humbly entreat;
I wait, blessed Lord, at Thy crucified feet;
By faith, for my cleansing, I see Thy blood flow;
Now wash me, and I shall be whiter than snow.

Used by arrangement with W. G. Fischer, owner of the copyright.

**97.**

A SINNER, Lord, behold I stand,
   In thought and word and deed;
But Jesus sits at thy right hand,
   For such to intercede.
From early infancy, I know,
   A rebel I have been;
And daily as I older grow,
   I fear I grow in sin.

But God can change this evil heart,
   And give a holy mind,
And His own heavenly grace impart,
   Which those who seek shall find.
Then let me all my sins confess,
   And pardoning grace implore,
That I may learn Thy righteousness,
   And love my Saviour more.

---

**98.**

INTO her chamber went
   A little child one day,
And by her chair she knelt,
   And thus began to pray:
Jesus, my eyes are closed,
   Thy form I cannot see—
If Thou art near me, Lord,
   Wilt Thou not speak to me?

I pray Thee, Lord, she said,
   That Thou wilt condescend
To stay within my heart,
   And ever be my Friend;

> The path of life looks dark—
> I would not go astray;
> Oh, let me have Thy hand
> To lead me in the way.

Words used by permission of Fletcher Osgood, owner of copyright.

---

**99.**

> Almighty God, Thy piercing eye
> Strikes through the shades of night,
> And our most secret actions lie
> All open to Thy sight.
> There's not a sin that we commit,
> Nor wicked word we say,
> But in Thy dreadful book 'tis writ
> Against the judgment day.
>
> Lord, at Thy feet ashamed I lie,
> Upward I dare not look;
> Pardon my sins before I die,
> And blot them from Thy book.
> Remember all the dying pains
> That my Redeemer felt,
> And let His blood wash out my stains
> And answer for my guilt.

---

**100.**

> Nearer, my God, to Thee,
> Nearer to Thee!
> E'en though it be a cross
> That raiseth me;
> Still all my song shall be
> Nearer, my God, to Thee,
> Nearer to Thee.

Though like a wanderer,
    The sun gone down,
Darkness be over me,
    My rest a stone;
Yet in my dreams I'd be
Nearer, my God, to Thee,
    Nearer to Thee!

There let the way appear
    Steps unto heaven;
All that Thou sendest me
    In mercy given;
Angels to beckon me
Nearer, my God, to Thee,
    Nearer to Thee!

Then, with my waking thoughts
    Bright with Thy praise,
Out of my stony griefs
    Bethels I'll raise;
So by my woes to be
Nearer, my God, to Thee,
    Nearer to Thee!

Or, if on joyful wing,
    Cleaving the sky,
Sun, moon and stars forgot,
    Upward I fly,
Still all my song shall be
Nearer, my God, to Thee,
    Nearer to Thee!

## 101.

Our Father who in Heaven art,
    All hallowed be Thy name :
Thy will be done on earth in love,
    As 'tis in heaven the same :
Give us this day our daily bread,
    That we on earth may live;
And teach us to forgive all ill;
    As Thou dost pardon give;
Help us when tempted to resist,
    All aid must come from Thee;
For Thine the kingdom and the power,
    And glory evermore shall be. Amen.

Copyright, 1896, by E. Revere.

---

## 102.

Our Father, which art in heaven, | hallowed | be Thy name :||
Thy kingdom come, Thy will be done on | earth, as it | is in heaven.||

Give us this | day our | daily | bread;||
And forgive us our trespasses, as we forgive | them that | trespass a- | gainst us.||

And lead us not into temptation, but de- | liver | us from | evil;||
For Thine is the kingdom, and the power, and the glory, for | ever. | Amen.||

---

## 103.

Jesus, tender Shepherd, hear me,
    Bless Thy little lamb to-night;
Through the darkness be Thou near me,
    Keep me safe till morning light.

All this day Thy hand hath led me,
  And I thank Thee for Thy care;
Thou hast clothed me, warmed me, fed me.—
  Listen to my evening prayer.

Let my sins be all forgiven;
  Bless the friends I love so well;
Take me, when I die, to heaven,
  Happy there with Thee to dwell.   Amen.

**104.**
God is in Heaven, can He hear
  A feeble prayer like mine?
Yes, little child, thou need'st not fear,
  He listeneth to thine.

God is in Heaven, can He see
  When I am doing wrong?
Yes, that He can, He looks at thee,
  All day and all night long.

God is in Heaven, would He know
  If I should tell a lie?
Yes, if thou saidst it very low,
  He'd hear it in the sky.

God is in Heaven, can I go
  To thank Him for His care?
Not yet, but love Him here below,
  And thou shalt praise Him there.

*Repeat after 1st verse.—*
  "I love them that love me; and those that seek me early shall find me."—Prov. 8: 17.

*Repeat after 2d verse.—*

"The eyes of the Lord *are* in every place."— Prov. 15: 3.

*Repeat after 3d verse.—*

"Lying lips *are* abomination to the Lord."—Prov. 12: 22.

*Repeat after 4th verse.—*

"If ye love me, keep my commandments."—John 14: 15.

---

**105.**

Jesus, lover of my soul,
  Let me to Thy bosom fly,
While the nearer waters roll,
  While the tempest still is high.

Hide me, O my Saviour, hide,
  Till the storm of life is past;
Safe into the haven guide,
  Oh, receive my soul at last.

Other refuge have I none,
  Hangs my helpless soul on Thee;
Leave, oh! leave me not alone,
  Still support and comfort me.

All my trust on Thee is stayed,
  All my help from Thee I bring;
Cover my defenceless head
  With the shadow of Thy wing.

Plenteous grace with Thee is found,
  Grace to pardon all my sin;
Let the healing streams abound,
  Make and keep me pure within.

Thou of life the fountain art,
  Freely let me take of Thee;
Spring Thou up within my heart,
  Rise to all eternity.

---

**106.**

The morning bright with rosy light,
  Has waked me from my sleep;
Father, I own Thy love alone
  Thy little one doth keep.

All through the day I humbly pray,
  Be Thou my guard and guide;
My sins forgive, and let me live,
  Blest Jesus near Thy side.

Oh, make Thy rest within my breast,
  Great Spirit of all grace;
Make me like Thee, then shall I be
  Prepared to see Thy face.

---

**107.**

I love Thee, Jesus,
  Oh, be my friend;
Watch me, and guide me
  To my life's end.
Jesus, my Saviour,
  Dwell in my heart,
And never let me
  From Thee depart.

Keep me, dear Saviour,
  True to Thy ways;
Tune my voice sweetly,
  To sing Thy praise.
When it shall please Thee
  Call me above,
Let me forever
  Dwell in Thy love.

Copyright, 1896, E. Revere.

---

**108.**
Come, Holy Spirit, heavenly Dove,
  With all Thy quickening powers,
Kindle a flame of sacred love
  In these cold hearts of ours.
Look, how we grovel here below,
  Fond of these trifling toys!
Our souls can neither fly nor go,
  To reach eternal joys.

In vain we tune our lifeless songs,
  In vain we strive to rise;
Hosannas languish on our tongues,
  And our devotion dies.
Come, Holy Spirit, heavenly Dove,
  With all Thy quickening powers
Come, shed abroad a Saviour's love,
  And that shall kindle ours.

---

**109.**
He's come! let ev'ry knee be bent,
  All hearts new joy resume;
Sing, ye redeemed, with one consent,
  "The Comforter is come."

What greater gift, what greater love,
    Could God on man bestow?
Angels for this rejoice above;
    Let man rejoice below.

Hail, blessed Spirit! may each soul
    Thy sacred influence feel;
Do Thou each sinful thought control,
    And fix our wavering zeal.

Thou to the conscience dost convey
    Those checks which we should know;
Thy motions point to us the way;
    Thou givest us strength to go.

---

**110.**

Holy Ghost, with light divine
Shine upon this heart of mine;
Chase the shades of night away,
Turn the darkness into day.

Holy Ghost, with power divine
Cleanse this guilty heart of mine;
Long has sin, without control,
Held dominion o'er my soul.

Holy Ghost, with joy divine
Cheer this saddened heart of mine;
Bid my many woes depart,
Heal my wounded, bleeding heart.

Holy Spirit, all divine,
Dwell within this heart of mine;
Cast down ev'ry idol throne—
Reign supreme, and reign alone.

**111.**

    THERE is a happy land,
        Far, far away,
    Where saints in glory stand,
        Bright, bright as day.
    Oh, how they sweetly sing,
    "Worthy is our Saviour King;"
    Loud let His praises ring,
        Praise, praise for aye.

    Come to that happy land,
        Come, come away,
    Why will ye doubting stand,
        Why still delay?
    Oh, we shall happy be,
    When, from sin and sorrow free,
    Lord, we shall dwell with Thee,
        Blest, blest for aye.

    Bright, in that happy land,
        Beams ev'ry eye:
    Kept by a Father's hand,
        Love cannot die.
    Oh, then to glory run;
    Be a crown and kingdom won;
    And bright, above the sun,
        We'll reign for aye.

---

**112.**

    I WANT to be an angel,
        And with the angels stand,
    A crown upon my forehead,
        A harp within my hand;

There, right before my Saviour,
  So glorious and so bright,
I'd wake the sweetest music,
  And praise Him day and night.


I never should be weary,
  Nor ever shed a tear,
Nor ever know a sorrow,
  Nor ever feel a fear;
But blessed, pure and holy,
  I'd dwell in Jesus' sight,
And with ten thousand thousands
  Praise Him both day and night.


I know I'm weak and sinful,
  But Jesus will forgive;
For many little children
  Have gone to Heaven to live.
Dear Saviour, when I languish,
  And lay me down to die,
Oh, send a shining angel
  To bear me to the sky.


Oh, there I'll be an angel,
  And with the angels stand,
A crown upon my forehead,
  A harp within my hand;
And there before my Saviour,
  So glorious and so bright,
I'll join the heavenly music,
  And praise Him day and night.

**113.**
    SAFE in the arms of Jesus,
      Safe on His gentle breast,
    There by His love o'ershaded,
      Sweetly my soul shall rest.
    Hark! 'tis the voice of angels,
      Born in a song to me,
    Over the fields of glory,
      Over the jasper sea.

CHO.—Safe in the arms of Jesus,
      Safe on His gentle breast,
    There by His love o'ershaded,
      Sweetly my soul shall rest.

    Safe in the arms of Jesus,
      Safe from corroding care,
    Safe from the world's temptations,
      Sin cannot harm me there.
    Free from the blight of sorrow,
      Free from my doubts and fears;
    Only a few more trials,
      Only a few more tears.

    Jesus, my heart's dear refuge,
      Jesus has died for me;
    Firm on the Rock of Ages,
      Ever my trust shall be.
    Here let me wait with patience,
      Wait till the night is o'er;
    Wait till I see the morning
      Break on the golden shore.

Copyright, 1870, by W. H. Doane, used by per.

## 114.

There's a land that is fairer than day,
　And by faith we can see it afar;
For the Father waits over the way,
　To prepare us a dwelling place there.

Chorus :—

　In the sweet by-and-by,
　　We shall meet on that beautiful shore,
　In the sweet by-and-by,
　　We shall meet on that beautiful shore.


We shall sing on that beautiful shore,
　The melodious songs of the blest,
And our spirits shall sorrow no more,
　Not a sigh for the blessing of rest.


To our bountiful Father above,
　We will offer our tribute of praise,
For the glorious gift of His love,
　And the blessings that hallow our days.

Used by arrangement with Oliver Ditson Co., owners of the copyright.

---

## 115.

Around the throne of God in heaven
　Thousands of children stand,—
Children whose sins are all forgiven,
　A holy, happy band,

Singing glory, glory, glory be to God on high.

In flowing robes of spotless white
  See ev'ryone arrayed,
Dwelling in everlasting light
  And joys that never fade,
    Singing, etc.

What brought them to that world above,
  That heaven so bright and fair,
Where all is joy and peace and love?
  How came those children there?
    Singing, etc.

Because the Saviour shed His blood
  To wash away their sin;
Bathed in that pure and precious flood,
  Behold them white and clean,
    Singing, etc.

On earth they sought the Saviour's grace,
  On earth they loved His name;
So now they see His precious face,
  And stand before the Lamb,
    Singing, etc.

---

### 116.

OVER the ocean wave, far, far away,
There the poor heathen live, waiting for day;
Groping in ignorance, dark as the night,
No blessed Bible to give them the light.

CHORUS :-
Pity them, pity them, Christians at home,
Haste with the bread of life, hasten and come.

Here in this happy land we have the light
Shining from God's own word, free, pure, and bright;
Shall we not send to them Bibles to read,
Teachers, and preachers, and all that they need?

Then, while the mission ships glad tidings bring,
List! as that heathen band joyfully sing,
"Over the ocean wave, oh, see them come,
Bringing the bread of life, guiding us home."
Copyright, 1883, by Biglow & Main, used by permission.

---

**117.**
THROW out the Life-Line across the dark wave,
There is a brother whom some one should save;
Somebody's brother! oh, who then, will dare
To throw out the Life-Line, his peril to share?

> CHORUS:—Throw out the Life-Line!
> Throw out the Life-Line!
> Some one is drifting away;
> Throw out the Life-Line!
> Throw out the Life-Line!
> Some one is sinking to-day.

Throw out the Life-Line with hand quick and strong:
Why do you tarry, why linger, so long?
See! he is sinking; oh, hasten to-day—
And out with the Life-Boat! away, then, away!

Throw out the Life-Line to danger-fraught men,
Sinking in anguish where you've never been:
Winds of temptation and billows of woe
Will soon hurl them out where the dark waters flow.

Soon will the season of rescue be o'er,
Soon will they drift to eternity's shore,
Haste then, my brother, no time for delay,
But throw out the Life-Line and save them to-day.
Copyright, 1890, by Biglow & Main, used by permission.

---

## 118.

I've thought of little children,
  Far off in heathen lands,
Taught how to worship idols
  And suffer at their hands.
I've heard them tell how mothers
  Would take their children dear,
And cast them in the water,
  Without a falling tear.
I've thought of little children,
  Far off in heathen lands,
Taught how to worship idols
  And suffer at their hands.

I'm told they have no Bible—
  No holy Sabbath day:
No teacher, friend, disciple,
  To teach them how to pray.
I'm told that they are ready
  To hear the gospel sound,
And I must give my penny,
  To send it all around.
I've thought of little children,
  Far off in heathen lands,
Taught how to worship idols
  And suffer at their hands.

I'm happy here, in concert
   With other children dear,
To send my offerings onward,
   To place a Bible there.
And may some friendly teacher,
   With Bible in his hand,
Be unto them a leader
   To Canaan's happy land.
I've thought of little children,
   Far off in heathen lands,
Taught how to worship idols
   And suffer at their hands.

---

**119.**

LITTLE builders all are we,
Builders for eternity,
Children of the mission bands
Working with our hearts and hands.
Building temples for our King
By the offerings we bring;
Living temples He doth raise,
Filled with life, and light, and praise.

One by one the stones we lay,
Building slowly day by day,
Building by our love are we
In the lands beyond the sea.
Building by each thought and prayer,
For the souls that suffer there;
Building in the Hindoo land,
Where the idols are as sand.

Building in Pacific Isles,
'Mid ruins wrought by Satan's wiles,
Building with our Father king
While our lips His praises sing.
And one day our eyes shall see
In a glad eternity;
Living stones, we helped to bring,
For the palace of our King.

---

**120.**
I HEAR the voices of children
   Calling from over the seas;
The wail of their pleading accents
   Comes borne upon ev'ry breeze.
And what are the children saying,
   Away in those heathen lands,
As they plaintively lift their voices,
   And eagerly stretch their hands?

REFRAIN:—Oh, listen! oh, listen!
   Oh, hear the children's cry!

"We grope in the midst of darkness—
   With none who can guide aright!
Oh, share with us, Christian children,
   A spark of your living light!"
This, this is the plaintive burden
   Borne hitherward on the breeze;
These, these are the words they are saying,
   Those children beyond the seas!

**121.**

    Go forth, ye heralds! in My name;
      Sweetly the gospel trumpet sound;
    The glorious jubilee proclaim,
      Where'er the human race is found.

    The joyful news to all impart,
      And teach them where salvation lies;
    With care bind up the broken heart,
      And wipe the tears from weeping eyes.

    Be wise as serpents, where you go,
      But harmless as the peaceful dove;
    And let your heaven-taught conduct show
      That you're commissioned from above.

    Freely from Me ye have received,
      Freely, in love, to others give;
    Thus shall your doctrines be believed,
      And, by your labors, sinners live.

---

**122.**

    I AM but a penny,
      From a little hand,
    Can I bear glad tidings
      Over all the land?
    Youthful love goes with me,
      So a penny's blest;
    God's love joined with children's
      Will do all the rest.

CHORUS:—Dropping, dropping, dropping,
      Hear us as we fall;
    Crowding in the mite-chest,
      Offerings great and small.

I'm a piece of silver,
    Worth ten cents they say,
Well that boy worked for me,
    Giving up his play,
Digging in the garden,
    Though he longed to run
Where his young companions
    Joined in boyish fun.

I'm a silver quarter,
    Little stitches neat,
And full many an errand
    Run by childish feet,
Earned me very bravely;
    Little girls can do
Noble work for missions,
    When they're good and true.

I'm a bright gold dollar,
    Ah! the child who died
Loved me 'mid her treasures,
    More than all beside;
One sad, mourning mother
    Held me very dear,
And my bright face glistens
    With her parting tear.

Surely God will bless us,
    As we gently fall;
Many prayers rise upward,
    For His help they call;
Till we form together
    Such a mighty band,
As to bear salvation
    Over all the land.

**123.**

    Far out upon the prairie
      How many children dwell,
   Who never read the Bible,
      Or hear the Sabbath bell;
   And when the holy morning
      Wakes us to sing and pray,
   They spend the precious moments
      In idleness and play.

Chorus:—Far out upon the prairie
      How many children dwell,
   Who never read the Bible,
      Or hear the Sabbath bell.

   For they have no kind pastor,
      Whose loving words have told
   Of Jesus, the good Shepherd,
      And called them to His fold;
   No Sabbath-school inviting
      Its pleasant doors within,
   No teacher's voice entreating
      To leave the way of sin.

   I wish that I could tell them
      How Jesus came to die,
   When He for little children
      Left His bright throne on high;
   And all the sad, sad story
      Of sorrow which He bore,
   When for His crown of glory
      A crown of thorns He wore.

And so each morn and evening,
  Whene'er I kneel in prayer,
I'll ask the gracious Saviour
  To send His gospel there;
That in the glorious city
  In which He dwells above,
We all may sing together
  Of His redeeming love.

## 124.

Have you ever brought a penny to the missionary box—
A penny which you might have spent like other little folks?
When it falls among the rest, have you ever heard a ring
Like a pleasant sound of welcome which the other pennies sing?

This is missionary music, and it has a pleasant sound,
For pennies make a shilling, and the shillings make a pound;
And many pounds together the Gospel news will send;
Which will tell the distant heathen that the Saviour is their Friend.

Oh! what happy, joyous music is the missionary song,
When it seems to come from ev'ry heart, and sounds from ev'ry tongue;
When happy Christian little ones all sing with one accord
Of the time when realms of darkness shall be kingdoms of the Lord!

Oh, but sweeter far than all which Jesus dearly loves to hear,
Are children's voices when they breathe a missionary prayer;
And many a one from distant lands will reach his Heavenly home
In answer to the children's prayer, "O Lord, Thy Kingdom come."

Then, missionary children, let this music never cease;
Work on, work on in earnest for the Lord, the Prince of Peace,
There is praying work and paying work for every heart and hand,
Till the Missionary chorus shall go forth through all the land.

---

**125.**

I AM a little Hindoo girl,
    Of Jesus never heard;
Oh, pity me, dear Christian child,
    Oh, send to me His word.
Oh, pity me, for I have grief
    So great I cannot tell,
And say if truly there's a heaven,
    Where such as I can dwell.

That pleading voice was borne across
    The rolling ocean wide,
Forthwith the children touched with love,
    Of Him who bled and died,
Said, here's our money, little girl,
    To buy God's word for you;
We wish 'twere more, a thousand fold,
    And you should have it too.

We've heard of Jesus, and we know
    The way of life full well;
Let children come to Me, He said,
    And they shall with Me dwell.
Ever with Him, with hearts renewed,
    And badness all forgiven;
For He who never fails has said,
    Of such the realm of heaven.

We'll speed the gospel o'er the earth,
    To each dear child so sad;
If one soul saved gives angels joy,
    Then will all heaven be glad.
And when at last we reach the shore,
    Where sorrow is unknown,
We hope to greet thee, Hindoo girl,
    Safe, safe before the throne.

---

## 126.

Should you wish to be told the best use of a penny,
I'll tell you a way that is better than any;
Not on apples, or cakes, or playthings to spend it,
But over the seas to the heathen to send it;
Come, listen to me, and I'll tell, if you please,
Of some poor little children far over the seas.

Their color is dark, for our God made them thus,
But He made them with bodies and feelings like us;
A soul too, that never will die has been given,
And there's room for these children with Jesus in
    heaven;
But who will now tell of such good things as these,
To the poor little heathen far over the seas.

Oh, think then of this, when a penny is given,
'Twill help a poor child on his way home to heaven;
Then give it to Jesus, and He will approve,
Nor scorn e'en the mite, if 'tis offered in love;
And oh, when in prayer you to Him bend your knees,
Remember the children far over the seas.

**127.**
  HEAR the pennies dropping,
   Listen while they fall,
  Ev'ry one for Jesus,
   He will get them all.

 REFRAIN. (Clap hands.)
  Dropping, dropping, dropping, dropping,
   Hear the pennies fall;
  Ev'ry one for Jesus,—
   He will get them all.

  Dropping, dropping ever,
   From each little hand,
  'Tis our gift to Jesus,
   From His little band.

  Now, while we are little,
   Pennies are our store,
  But, when we are older,
   Lord, we'll give Thee more.

  Though we have not money,
   We can give Him love,
  He will own our offering,
   Smiling from above.

From Dew Drops, by permission of John J. Hood.

**128.**

Oh, send forth the Bible, more precious than gold!
Let no one presume, the best gift to withhold;
It speaks to all nations in language so plain
That he who will read it, true wisdom may gain.

It points us to heaven, where the righteous will go,
It warns us to shun the dark regions of woe:
It shows us the evil and dangers of sin,
And opens a fountain for cleansing within.

It tells us of one who is mighty to save,
Who died on the cross, and arose from the grave;
Who dwelleth on high, in that holy abode,
Interceding for man with a pardoning God.

It tells us that all will awake from the tomb,
Bid sinners reflect on a judgment to come;
It tells us that mansions of bliss are prepared,
The hope of believers,—their glorious reward.

Oh, who would neglect such a volume as this
That warns us from danger, invites us to bliss?
Send forth the blest Bible, earth's regions around,
Wherever the footsteps of man shall be found.

---

**129.**

Sing a song of jugs to-night,
Nickel, dime and penny,
When we count the nickels o'er
We hope there will be many.

Cho.—Jingle! jingle! jingle! jugs,
See the money flying
Hurrah! hurrah! for ev'ry one,
Who's for missions trying.

We have worked like busy bees
　When they gather honey,
And we thank our friends to-night
　For all their help and money.

Break the jugs, with right good-will,
　'Tis the time of clover;
When our teacher said, that we
　Should count the money over.

When we count the money o'er,
　And the jugs are broken,
Missions then, will surely have
　Of our good-will, a token.

Copyright, 1896, by E. Revere.

---

**130.**

Out in the western wild
Roams the poor Indian,
Without a teacher kind
To tell him of salvation;
No blessed Bible there,
Speaking of the Saviour
Who died that we might live
In happiness forever.

Oh, send the Bible then
To those poor Indian children,
Preachers and teachers dear,
To lead their souls to heaven;
Then when we reach that home,
Where we shall live forever,
We may meet those children there,
And praise the Lord together.

**131.**

Only a single penny,
   'Tis all I have to give,
But yet, when more are added,
   'Twill help some one to live.

Chorus :—Only the little pennies,
   Dropping one by one,
Gather them in the mite-box,
   Till Christ's kingdom's won.

Only a single penny,
   Saved from a slender store,
Will truly be accepted,
   If we can give no more.

Only a single penny,
   Yet now with comfort sweet,
Fearing no scorn we lay it
   Down at the Saviour's feet.

From Bud & Blossoms, copyrighted by the Emma Pitt Pub. Co., Baltimore, Md.

---

**132.**

There is something on earth for the children to do,
   For the child that is striving to be
Like the One who once murmured in accents of love,
   "Let the little ones come unto Me."

Full Chorus :—
There is something to do, there is something to do ;
   There is something for children to do ;
On the beautiful earth where the Saviour had birth,
   There is something for children to do.

There are sweet winning words to the weary and sad,
  By their glad loving lips to be said ;
There are hearts that are waiting by some little hand,
  Unto Jesus, the Lord to be led.

There are lessons to learn both at home and at school ;
  There are battles to fight for the right ;
There's a watch to be kept over temper and tongue,
  And God's help to be asked day and night.

There are smiles to be given, kind deeds to be done,
  Gentle words to be dropped by the way—
For the child that is seeking to follow the Lord,
  There is something to do ev'ry day.

Copyright, 1883, by Biglow & Main, used by permission.

---

**133.**

I cannot do great things for God,
  Who did so much for me,
But I would like to show my love,
  Dear Jesus, unto Thee ;
Faithful in ev'ry little thing,
  O Saviour, may I be.

There are small crosses I may take,
  Small burdens I may bear,
Small acts of faith and deeds of love,
  Small sorrows I may share ;
And little bits of work for Thee,
  I may do ev'rywhere.

And so I ask Thee give me grace,
  My little place to fill,
That I may ever walk with Thee,
  And ever do Thy will;
And in each duty, great or small,
  I may be faithful still.

---

**134.**
"Give," said the little stream,
  (Give, oh give, give, oh give,)
"Give," said the little stream,
  As it hurried down the hill;
"I am small, I know, but wherever I go,
  (Give, oh give, give, oh give,)
I am small, I know, but wherever I go,
  The fields grow greener still."

Refrain:—
  Singing, singing all the day,
  Give away, oh, give away,
  Singing, singing all the day,
  Give, oh, give away.

"Give," said the little rain,
  (Give, oh give, give, oh give,)
"Give," said the little rain,
  As it fell upon the flowers;
"I will raise the drooping heads again,
  (Give, oh give, give, oh give,)
I will raise the drooping heads again,
  And freshen the summer bowers."

"Give," said the violet sweet,
    (Give, oh give, give, oh give,)
"Give," said the violet sweet,
    In its gentle, springlike voice;
"From cot and hall they will hear my call,
    (Give, oh give, give, oh give,)
From cot and hall they will hear my call,
    They will find me and rejoice."

Give then, for Jesus give,
    (Give, oh give, give, oh give,)
Give then, for Jesus give,
    There is something all can give;
Oh, do as the streams and the blossoms do,
    (Give, oh give, give, oh give,)
Oh, do as the streams and the blossoms do,
    And for God and others live.

Copyright, 1883, by Biglow & Main, used by permission.

---

## 135.

To our dear Sabbath-school there ought many to come,
Who spend Sunday wandering or trifling at home;
So I'll try to bring one, or I'll try to bring two,
Yes, all that I can I'm determined to do.

God meant all the people who live in this place,
To hear of His goodness and join in His praise;
So I'll try to bring one, or I'll try to bring two,
Yes, all that I can I'm determined to do.

Out there in the lot that I pass ev'ry day,
How many spend Sunday in frolic or play;
If I could get one of those boys now, or two,
To come here next Sabbath, what good it might do.

Perhaps up to heaven some day I may go,
What glory and blessedness then I shall know;
But I want in that glory that many may share,
That one, two, yes, all I can take may be there.

---

**136.**

Give to Jesus, give to Jesus,
  Give to Jesus just now;
Just now give to Jesus,
  Give to Jesus just now.

Give your pennies, give your pennies,
  Give your pennies just now;
Just now give your pennies,
  Give your pennies just now.

Give to others, give to others,
  Give to others just now;
Just now give to others,
  Give to others just now.

4. Give all freely.
5. Send the Bible.
6. Send the teachers.
7. Save the heathen.
8. Tell of Jesus.
9. Jesus loves them.
10. Died to save them.
11. Ask His blessing.

## 137.

(The 1st verse should be sung by six children, other verses are sung by whole school.)

DEAR little children, please give to me
Some of your pennies, that I may see,
And read the Bible, God's holy word.
Oh, send us tidings of His dear love!

Yes, little children, we want to send
The gospel tidings to the world's end;
We know that Jesus from His bright home
Still cares for you, though from Him you roam.

We hope to greet you in Heaven above,
Resting with Jesus where all is love;
When we send pennies we'll breathe a prayer
That you will love Him and meet us there.

Copyright, 1896, by E. Revere.

---

## 138.

SOFTLY, softly through the midnight,
   Let the bells their message ring;
All the earth is hushed and silent,
   'Tis the birth-night of the King.
In a manger poor and lowly,
   Was the Christ child's cradle nest;
He, the Ruler, Lord, and Saviour,
   In no royal robe was drest.

Only Bethlehem shepherds watching,
   By their flocks upon the hill,
Heard the hosts of angels singing,
   "Peace on earth, on earth good will."

Strange the silent world could slumber,
  Strange that city, quaint and still,
Felt no deeper pulse awaken,
  Felt no higher, holier thrill!

And the busy throng moved onward,
  Knowing not, and heeding less,
Now the world kneels, trusting, prayerful,
  Knowing that He came to bless.
Gladly, gladly through the stillness,
  Let the joyful message ring;
He hath loved us, He hath saved us,
  He through endless time is King.

---

## 139.

AND there were in the same country shepherds *abiding* | in the | field,‖
Keeping watch *over* their flock by | night,‖
And, lo! the angel of the *Lord* came upon them, | *and* the glory of the *Lord* shone round about them; and they were | *sore* a- | fraid.‖
And the angel said unto them, |
Fear *not:* | for, *behold*, I bring *you* good | tidings of great | joy, | which shall *be* to | all | people.‖
For unto you is born this day in the city of | David a | Saviour, which is | Christ the Lord.‖
And this shall be a *sign* | unto | you;‖
Ye shall find the babe *wrapped* in | swaddling clothes, | lying in a | manger.‖
And suddenly there was with the *angel* a multitude *of* the | heavenly host | praising *God*, | and saying,‖
Glory to God in the highest, and on earth peace, good will toward men.‖A- | men.‖

**140.**

List to the bells of Christmas!
   What is the news they ring?
List to the children's anthem!
   What are the words they sing?
This is the bells glad message,
   This is the children's song:
Lo! in the Bethlehem village
   Jesus, the Lord is born.

"Joy to the world!" the bells chime;
   "Good will," the children sing;
"Jesus is born; our Saviour;
   Jesus, Redeemer, King.
He who came down from heaven,
   Dying that we might live,
He who His dear self gave us,
   Teaching us how to give."

This is the bells, glad message,
   This is the children's song,
Echoing down through the ages
   On each glad Christmas morn!
"Joy to the world!" the bells chime;
   "Good will," the children sing;
"Jesus is born; our Saviour;
   Jesus, Redeemer, King."

---

**141.**

Long, long ago in a manger low,
   Was cradled from above,
A little child, in whom God smiled,
   A Christmas gift of love;
When hearts were bitter and unjust,
   And cruel hands were strong,
The noise He hushed with hope and trust,
   And peace began her song.

Where'er the Father's Christmas gifts
    Seem only frost and snow,
And anxious stress and loneliness,
    And poverty and woe;
Straightway provide, a welcome wide,
    Nor wonder why they came;
They stand outside our hearts and bide,
    Knocking in Jesus' name.

For trouble, cold, and dreary care
    Are angels in disguise,
And greeted fair, with trust and prayer,
    As peace and love they rise;
They are the manger, wide and low,
    In which a Christ child lies;
O welcome Guest, Thy cradle nest,
    Is always God's surprise.

**142.**

HARK! the merry, merry bells,
    Christmas chimes are ringing;
Each the same glad story tells,
    Angel hosts were singing.
When on far Judea's plain,
Shepherds heard their sweet refrain,
From the welkin ringing,
From the welkin ringing.

Peace on earth, good will to men,
    Tidings glad they're telling;
Blessed Christmas come again,
    On the air is swelling.
Now let notes of praise ascend,
Voices altogether blend,
Joy fill ev'ry dwelling,
Joy fill ev'ry dwelling.

Christ is born, the Prince of Peace,
    Bells are now repeating;
Let all strife and discord cease,
    Give all kindly greeting.
Let this day of Jesus' birth
Bind together hearts on earth,
Time is all too fleeting,
Time is all too fleeting.

---

**143.**

A STAR shone in the heavens
    On Christmas morn,
Above the place where Jesus,
    The Lord, was born.

CHO.—O holy, holy Christmas,
    O blessed, blessed Christmas,
O joyful, joyful Christmas,
    When Christ was born.

The wise men saw its brightness,
    And came from far,
They found the way to Jesus,
    Led by the star.

Oh, may this star of beauty
    Still point the way
To lead us all to Jesus,
    This Christmas day.

Used by permission of D. C. Cook Pub. Co., owners of copyright.

**144.**

    Cheerily hail the Christmas morn,
      Carol a tuneful lay;
    Welcome the infant Saviour born,
      Greet Him with joy to-day.

Cho.—Merrily now the bells we hear,
      Chiming in chorus sweet and clear;
    Gather and sing, gather and sing,
      Welcome the children's King.

    Wonderful song of holy mirth
      Sweeping along the sky,
    Glory to God and peace on earth,
      Glory to God on high.

    Over the world good news proclaim
      Heralds of love, away;
    Jesus the Lord has come to reign,
      Tell it with joy to-day.

---

**145.**

    'Round our sparkling Christmas tree,
      Let our gladsome voices ring;
    Children of the Lord are we,
      In His praise our hymn we sing.

Cho.—Glory be to God on high,
      Peace on earth, good will to men;
    Let us join the angel band,
      Shout aloud the glad refrain.

    Thanks to Him whose tender love
      In the wintry midnight wild,
    Sent the Saviour from above,
      Gentle Jesus, holy child.

Heaven with joy and music rang,
  Silvery stars broke silence then;
Angel voices greeting sang—
  Peace on earth, good will to men.

Now once more the night comes round,
  Now the hour once more draws near;
When that anthem's holy sound,
  Falls on fancy's listening ear.

On our hearts, oh let it thrill,
  Jesus there be born again;
And with peace our bosoms fill,
  Peace on earth, good will to men.

---

**146.**
O JOYFUL bells of Christmas-tide,
  The dear old story tell,
How long ago a bright new star
In heaven was seen, and from afar
The wise men brought to Him they sought
  The child Emmanuel.
O joyful bells of Christmas-tide,
  The dear old story tell.

O joyful bells of Christmas-tide,
  Repeat the wondrous tale,
How long ago to shepherds came
An angel choir, and while aflame
With heaven's own light the skies are bright,
  The Christ child's coming hail.
O joyful bells of Christmas-tide,
  Repeat the wondrous tale.

O joyful bells of Christmas-tide,
    Ring out, ring out again,
How long ago a Saviour's birth,
Good will and peace began on earth;
Good will and peace no more to cease,
    From heaven to sinful men.
O joyful bells of Christmas-tide,
    Ring out, ring out again.

## 147.

The anthem the angels were singing,
    O'er Bethlehem's plains long ago,
Still down through the ages ringing,
    The comfort of millions below;
The anthem of joy and salvation,
    Of love to a sin-stricken race,
To every kindred and nation,
    Good will from the Father of peace.

The star which the wise men was guiding,
    O'er far distant lands long ago,
Is still in the heavens abiding,
    The holy child Jesus to show;
Inviting the world to adore Him,
    To bow like the magi of old,
And cast down their treasures before Him,
    The heart's purest incense and gold.

We gather this festival evening,
    Our Lord and our Saviour to seek,
With garlands His temple adorning,
    With praises His goodness to speak,
Far more than the shepherd or wise men
    We long the dear Saviour to see,
For He has said: Suffer the children,
    The children to come unto Me.

**148.**

Hark! the angels singing,
  Wake the happy morn!
Joyful tidings bringing,
  Christ the Lord is born!
In a lowly manger,
  This shall be the sign;
See the newborn stranger,
  Hail the Babe divine!

Solo:—Sisters dear and brothers,
  Sing, oh, sing away;
This above all others,
  Is the children's day;
Hear its blessed story,
  Once as young as we,
Christ the Prince of glory,
  Slept on Mary's knee.

Hark! the angels singing,
  Wake the happy morn!
Joyful tidings bringing,
  Christ the Lord is born!
In a lowly manger,
  This shall be the sign;
See the newborn stranger,
  Hail the Babe divine!

Solo:—Where's a chorus meeter,
  For His advent here?
Where a carol sweeter,
  To his gentle ear?
None can come so near Him,
  Him the undefiled,
None so love and fear Him,
  As a Christian child.

**149.**

    Hail to the morn
    When Christ was born,
Did ever break such glorious dawn?
    When heaven's light,
    All clear and bright,
Shone down upon sin's darkest night.

    Angels on high
    Broke through the sky,
To peal the song of victory,
    Glory to God!
    They sound abroad,
Peace and good will through Christ the Lord.

    For Jesus came,
    Oh, glorious name!
To save our race from sin and shame;
    In lowly birth
    He came to earth,
God's gift, than all beside, more worth.

    Sing, children sing,
    Bring, children bring
Your best, your richest offering:
    And o'er again,
    Repeat the strain,
Christ comes to rescue sinful men.

---

**150.**

    Gleam out, oh, Christmas brightness,
      It is our holy day!
    Shine down in radiant gladness,
      With clear and heavenly ray.

Go forth, our Christmas carols,
   With blessing-laden wing,
And bear to listening mortals
   The strains the angels sing.


Shine out, bright stars of Christmas,
   And as an anthem sweet,
To earth's remotest nations,
   Our Saviour's love repeat.
Ring out, oh, childish voices,
   A glad and joyous hymn,
For Christ, the children's Saviour,
   Was born in Bethlehem.

---

**151.**

LITTLE children, can you tell,
Do you know the story well,
Why the angels sang for joy,
On the Christmas morn?
Shepherds sat upon the ground,
Fleecy flocks were scattered round,
When an angel bright came down,
On the Christmas morn.

Joy and peace the angels sang,
Far the pleasant echoes rang;
Peace on earth, good will to man!
On the Christmas morn.
For a little Babe that day,
Lowly in a manger lay,
Born on earth, our Lord to be,
On the Christmas morn.

Let us sing the angels' song,
And the pleasant sounds prolong,
To this Babe of Bethlehem,
On the Christmas morn.
Peace, our youthful hearts shall fill,
Peace on earth, to men good will!
Thus we'll sing with angels still,
On the Christmas morn.

---

**152.**

To us this day in David's town,
A Saviour, Christ the Lord is born;
The heavenly host announce his birth,
Sing, O ye heavens, rejoice, O earth!

CHORUS:—

O Bethlehem! O Bethlehem!
The Child is born in Bethlehem;
Glory to God, in highest strain,
Jesus is born in Bethlehem;
The shining ones with songs descend,
Good will to men, no more to end.

The Wonderful in infant guise,
The Son of God in manger lies;
Angels awake the glad refrain,
Sweet peace on earth, good will to men!

The Prince of Peace at Bethlehem,
The shepherds view with gladsome mein
Glory to God, in highest strain,
On earth be peace, good will to men!

**153.**
　　Merry, merry Christmas ev'rywhere!
　　Cheerily it ringeth through the air;
　　Christmas bells, Christmas trees,
　　Christmas odors on the breeze.
　　Merry, merry Christmas ev'rywhere!
　　Cheerily it ringeth through the air;
　　Why should we so joyfully
　　Sing with grateful mirth?
　　See! the Sun of Righteousness
　　Beams upon the earth!


　　Merry, merry Christmas ev'rywhere!
　　Cheerily it ringeth through the air;
　　Christmas bells, Christmas trees,
　　Christmas odors on the breeze.
　　Merry, merry Christmas ev'rywhere!
　　Cheerily it ringeth through the air;
　　Light for weary wanderers,
　　Comfort for th' oppressed!
　　He will guide His trusting ones
　　Into perfect rest.


　　Merry, merry Christmas ev'rywhere!
　　Cheerily it ringeth through the air;
　　Christmas bells, Christmas trees,
　　Christmas odors on the breeze.
　　Merry, merry Christmas ev'rywhere!
　　Cheerily it ringeth through the air;
　　Deeds of Faith and Charity;
　　These our offerings be,
　　Leading ev'ry soul to sing,
　　Christ was born for me!

Copyright, 1870, by Biglow & Main, used by permission.

**154.**

In a country far away,
Sleeping in a manger, lay
One so holy, One so mild,
Jesus, blessed Christmas-child.
He was born upon this day,
In David's town so far away,
He the good and loving One,
Mary's ever blessed Son.
Let us all our voices lend,
For He was the children's friend,
He so lovely, He so mild,
Jesus, blessed Christmas-child.

Shepherds watching flocks at night,
Saw a clear and heavenly light;
Bells of David's town rang clear,
Bringing peace and Christmas-cheer;
Angels sang their anthems sweet,
Wise men worshipped at His feet,
Brought their gifts from near and far,
Guided by the Eastern Star.
Let us all our voices lend,
For He was the children's friend,
He so lovely, He so mild,
Jesus, blessed Christmas-child.

Used by arrangement with Oliver Ditson Co., owners of the copyright.

---

**155.**

Ring the bells, the Christmas bells,
　Chime out the wondrous story;
First in song, on angel tongues,
　It came from realms of glory;

"Peace on earth, good will to men,"
   Angelic voices ringing,
Christ, the Lord, to earth has come,
   His glorious message bringing.

CHORUS :—
   Ring the bells, the merry Christmas bells;
     Chime out the wondrous story,
   Glory be to God on high,
     Forevermore be glory.

Wise men hastened from the East,
   To bring their richest treasure;
Gold, and myrrh, and frankincense,
   And jewels without measure;
Him they sought, although a king,
   They found among the lowly,
In the Virgin's arms He lay
   The Babe so pure and holy.

Earthly crowns were not for Him,
   He came God's love revealing;
On the cross He died for us,
   His blood forgiveness sealing;
'Tis the Saviour promised long,
   Ring out your loudest praises;
Ev'ry heart this happy day,
   Its grateful anthem raises.

Copyright, 1883, by Biglow & Main, used by permission.

---

## 156.

WHILE shepherds watched their flocks by night,
   All seated on the ground,
The angel of the Lord came down,
   And glory shone around,
   And glory shone around.

"Fear not," said He, for mighty dread
    Had seized their troubled mind;
"Glad tidings of great joy I bring
    To you and all mankind,
    To you and all mankind."


"To you, in David's town, this day
    Is born, of David's line,
The Saviour, who is Christ, the Lord;
    And this shall be the sign,
    And this shall be the sign:


"The heavenly Babe you there shall find,
    To human view displayed,
All meanly wrapt in swathing bands,
    And in a manger laid,
    And in a manger laid."


Thus spake the seraph; and forthwith
    Appeared a shining throng
Of angels, praising God, who thus
    Addressed their joyful song,
    Addressed their joyful song.


"All glory be to God on high,
    And on the earth be peace;
Good will henceforth, from heaven to men,
    Begin, and never cease,
    Begin, and never cease!"

**157.**
    Banish gloom and sadness,
      Banish grief and care;
    Bid bright joy and gladness
      Welcome ev'rywhere.
    Ev'ry burden lighten,
      Sorrow, must depart;
    Christmas joys should brighten
      Ev'ry Christian's heart.

CHORUS:—Peace! peace on earth,
      Good will to man be given;
    All hail the blessed birth
      Of Christ, the King of Heaven.

    Christmas bells are ringing,
      Calling us to raise,
    High in tuneful singing,
      Thankful hymns of praise.
    All, both high and lowly,
      Should alike rejoice;
    And in service holy
      Join with heart and voice.

    Christmas, happy Christmas!
      Herald of good will,
    Come with songs of glory
      Bright with gladness still.
    Peace and hope may brighten,
      Patient love may glow;
    Christmas bells are ringing,
      As in years ago.

**158.**

He is coming! He is coming!
  Rise, O herald of His birth!
Rise, O Light of lights, illuming
  All the darkness of the earth.
He is coming! He is coming!
  All the sky with glory glows,
And each desert place is blooming
  Into beauty like a rose.

He is coming to deliver
  All the nations by His birth!
He is coming, Christ, the giver
  Of salvation, to the earth.
God hath spoken, God hath spoken,
  Wake, ye people, wake and sing!
While ye wait the promised token
  Of the coming of the King.

---

**159.**

Christ was born in Bethlehem,
Christ was born in Bethlehem,
Christ was born in Bethlehem,
And in a manger lay,
And in a manger lay;
Christ was born in Bethlehem,
And in a manger lay.

Sinners crucified Him,
Sinners crucified Him,
Sinners crucified Him,
They nailed Him to the cross,
They nailed Him to the cross;
Sinners crucified Him,
They nailed Him to the cross.

Joseph begged the body,
Joseph begged the body,
Joseph begged the body,
And laid it in the tomb,
And laid it in the tomb;
Joseph begged the body,
And laid it in the tomb.


Mary came in sorrow,
Mary came in sorrow,
Mary came in sorrow,
Her loving Lord to see,
Her loving Lord to see;
Mary came in sorrow,
Her loving Lord to see.


Down came an angel,
Down came an angel,
Down came an angel,
And rolled the stone away,
And rolled the stone away;
Down came an angel,
And rolled the stone away.


(Children clap hands.)

Shout, shout the victory!
Shout, shout the victory!
Shout, shout the victory!
Our Lord is risen to-day,
Our Lord is risen to-day;
Shout, shout the victory!
Our Lord is risen to-day.

**160.**

"Unto us a Child is born,"
  Sing, children, sing to-day!
Wake, oh earth, this happy morn,
  Join our Christmas lay.
"Tidings of great joy" we sing,
  Sing, children, sing to-day!
Angels came the news to bring;
  Angels join our lay.

"To all people it shall be,"
  Sing, children, sing to-day!
Earth's glad song of jubilee,
  All men join our lay.
"Peace on earth, good will to men,"
  Sing, children, sing to-day!
Christ has come to save from sin,
  Join our Christmas lay.

Prince of Peace, oh, blessed name!
  Sing, children, sing to-day!
Tell the nations why He came;
  They will join our lay.
Prince of Peace, our Saviour King,
  Sing, children, sing to-day!
Loving hearts and lives we bring
  With our Christmas lay.

---

**161.**

Hark, I hear the angel voices,
  Sweetly ringing through the sky,
Pealing forth the royal chorus,
  Glory be to God on high.

Cho.—Sing hosanna, glad hosanna,
    Join with them this Christmas morn;
Heaven and earth repeat the story,
    Christ the Lord to-day is born.

List how sweet the angel voices
    Chant it through the silent air;
Christ is born, the King of glory,
    Born that we His love might share.

Sing! oh, sing like angel voices,
    Thrilling notes of love to swell;
Herald forth the gladsome morning,
    Tidings full of joy to tell.

Christ is born our mighty Saviour,
    Oh, proclaim the news afar!
Still it shines with beams of glory,
    Bethlehem's bright and cheering star.

---

**162.**
    Cheerily, cheerily sing once more,
        Jesus the Lord is born;
Carry the message from shore to shore,
    Jesus the Lord is born.

Cho.—Love is folding her snow-white wings,
    Peace, good will to the world she brings;
Sweetly now to her harp she sings,
    Jesus the Lord is born.

Voices are calling away, away,
    Jesus the Lord is born;
Joyfully, tenderly, hark they say,
    Jesus the Lord is born.

Now in the chime of bells we hear,
 Jesus the Lord is born;
List to their melody, loud and clear,
 Jesus the Lord is born.

Gladly we gather, our hearts to raise,
 Jesus the Lord is born;
Gladly we mingle our songs of praise,
 Jesus the Lord is born.

---

## 163.

MAGI.—Boys.
 We saw a star, a bright new star,
  In yonder Eastern skies;
 It led us from a country far,
  To where Emmanuel lies.

ALL.
CHO.—Emmanuel! Emmanuel!
  His praises now outpour;
 Emmanuel! Emmanuel!
  God with us ever more!

SHEPHERDS.—Girls.
 We heard a song, an angel song,
  Float sweetly o'er the plain;
 The Prince of Peace, expected long,
  To-night begins His reign.

ALL.
CHO.—O Prince of Peace! O Prince of Peace!
  The law of love is Thine;
 O Prince of Peace! O Prince of Peace!
  Reign in this heart of mine.

**164.**

    Through the blue and starry heavens
        Came the angels robed in white;
    Shepherds heard the glorious anthem,
        Wise men saw the Christmas light.

Chorus:—

    "Christ is born," the bells are telling,
        "Peace on earth," they seem to say;
    And our hearts with joy are swelling,
        Christ is born! 'tis Christmas day!

    Chime, ye bells, the sweetest music,
        Send your message far and wide;
    'Tis the Christ-child come to bless us;
        In our hearts let peace abide

    Ring, ye bells, with joy repeating
        All the sweet and glad refrain;
    Christ is born, our blessed Saviour,
        So that we new life may gain.

    Peace on earth, good will to all men,
        May God's grace around us cling;
    Christ is born to save and bless us,
        Our Redeemer, Lord and King.

    Sing in praise, ye little children,
        Let your voices sweetly blend.
    May your hearts be filled with gladness,
        Christ is born! the children's Friend!

**165.**
MERRY Christmas bells are ringing,
  Ringing far and near;
Angels' voices sweetly singing,
  Singing high and clear.
Glory! for the Lord is come,
  Jesus makes the earth His home.
Glory! for the Lord is come,
  Jesus makes the earth His home.

Happy voices catch the echo
  Of the angels' song;
Grand old chant, and joyous carol,
  Ring the aisles along.
Let our lips their homage pay,
  To the Saviour born to-day.
Let our lips their homage pay,
  To the Saviour born to-day.

Precious Christmas gifts are gladdening
  Many a heart and home;
But the gift, all gifts excelling,
  Christ Himself is come.
In your hearts make speedy room,
  For the Christ, the Lord is come.
In your hearts make speedy room,
  For the Christ, the Lord is come.

And have we no gifts to offer
  To our Lord and King?
Lord, ourselves, our souls and bodies,
  Unto Thee we bring.
With our lives glad homage pay,
  To the Saviour born to-day.
With our lives glad homage pay,
  To the Saviour born to-day.

**166.**

Wakeful shepherds, long ago,
  Watching on the lonely plain,
Listening in the silent night,
  Heard a soft and sweet refrain;
Heavenly music filled the air,
  Swiftly holy angels fly,
Singing as they downward sweep,
  Glory be to God on high.

Filled with awe the shepherds sat,
  Nearer came the heavenly throng,
While the mountains, vales and hills
  Echoed back their glorious song;
Peace on earth, to men good will,
  On this sacred Christmas morn,
Tidings of great joy we bring,
  For your Saviour Christ is born.

Jesus in a manger lay,
  Humble as the feeblest child,
And through life was always pure,
  Gentle, loving, meek and mild;
Till upon the cross He died,
  Bringing our salvation nigh;
Let us sing with grateful hearts,
  Glory be to God on high.

---

**167.**

Ques:—Tell me why is Christmas day
  The day for songs and mirth?
Ans:—It calls to mind the happiest,
  That ever dawned on earth,
The day when God sent angels down
  To sing the Saviour's birth.

QUES:—What's the song for Christmas day,
  The glad, the sweet refrain?
ANS:—Glory to God in heaven above,
  Peace and good will to men;
  Let all the joy-bells peal it out,
  Again and yet again.

QUES:—How shall children keep the day
  To please their Lord above?
ANS:—By singing songs of thankfulness,
  And doing deeds of love;
  By bearing high the olive branch
  Of peace, like Noah's dove.

QUES:—Will He let such little ones
  His wondrous mercy tell?
ANS:—Yes, we may carry wide the news,
  And it will please Him well;
  The blessed news that Jesus came
  To save our souls from hell.

---

**168.**

WHAT do we find in the manger,
 On this sacred morn?
Lo! a precious stranger,
 Jesus Christ is born!

CHO:—Glory, glory be to God on high!
  Glory, glory be to God on high!

Bethlehem of Judea
 Is the chosen place
Where the Infant Treasure
 Comes to bless our race.

Shepherds, with fear and trembling,
   Hear an Angel voice
Bearing gladsome tidings,
   Bidding them rejoice.

Spices and costly tribute,
   Choicest gifts of gold,
Are, in free oblation,
   Brought by men of old.

We will give adoration,
   Hearts of fervent love,
Telling every nation,
   Jesus reigns above!

Copyright, 1870, by Biglow & Main, used by permission.

---

**169.**

   GLORY in the highest!
Ring the children's voices;
   Full of happy wonder,
Heart with heart rejoices;
For the Christ-child comes to-day,
With the babes of earth to play.

   Glory in the highest!
Murmur tearful voices;
   Yea, despite its sorrow,
Now the earth rejoices;
For the Christ-child's holy face
Sweetest shines in saddest place.

Glory in the highest!
Chant adoring voices;
In our Father's temple,
Heaven with earth rejoices;
Men and angels caroling,
"Crown the Christ-child Lord and King."

---

## 170.

List, a thousand birds are singing,
Cross the hills and meads away;
And a thousand leaves are bursting,
From their darkness into day.

Chorus :—
All the bells shall tell the story,
In this sacred theme agreed;
Praise to God! to God the glory!
Christ the Lord is risen indeed.

Life is on the breath of morning,
Life is in the open sky;
Peace is in the heart's glad throbbing,
Peace is in the wind's low sigh.

Peace is in the creamy lilies,
Why may we not also say,
Peace hath its contented biding
In our hearts, a calm to-day?

May we learn the simple lesson,
They that toil not, neither spin;
This, to be content with living,
If our hearts are pure within.

Words copyrighted by the Emma Pitt Pub. Co., Baltimore, Md.

## 171.

Gather, children, gather,
    Fragrant offerings bring;
Carol, children, carol,
    Gladsome carols sing!
Angel choirs are singing,
    In the early dawn;
Jesus Christ is risen,
    Glorious Easter morn!
Hallelujah, hallelujah,
    Amen, amen.

Come and give to Jesus,
    Risen from the tomb,
Wreaths of sweetest flowers,
    Nature's Easter bloom;
Hare bells ringing sweetly,
    Lilies singing joy;
Roses breathing incense,
    Praise without alloy.
Hallelujah, hallelujah,
    Amen, amen.

## 172.

Shout, shout aloud the tidings of Redemption;
    Peal, merry bells, the anthem of the free;
Clap, clap your hands, and sing for joy, ye people,
    Death hath been vanquished, his terrors now flee.

Chorus:—
    Sound the timbrel, clash the cymbal,
        Ring the joyous Easter chime;
    Join our voices in the chorus,
        Swell the melody sublime.

See, see, the tomb holds but the linen swathings;
  Joy! joy! the earth cannot retain our King;
Join, join to tell His wondrous resurrection;
  Sing of His mighty power salvation to bring.

Sing, sing the words by watching angels spoken,
  Jesus is risen; behold, He is not here;
Come, see the place where our dear Lord lay sleeping;
  Death for His loving ones hath never more fear.

**Used by permission of John J. Hood, owner of copyright.**

---

**173.**
  The little flowers came from the ground,
    At Easter-time! at Easter-time!
  They raised their heads and looked around,
    At happy Easter-time;
  And seemed each little bud to say,
  All people bless this holy day,
  For Christ is risen, the angels say,
  This holy Easter day, this holy Easter day.

  The pure white lily raised its cup,
    At Easter-time! at Easter-time!
  The crocus to the sky looked up,
    At happy Easter-time;
  Oh, hear the song of heaven, they say
  Its glory shines in us to-day,
  Oh, may it shine in us alway,
  At holy Easter-time, at holy Easter-time.

  'Twas long ago, 'twas long ago,
    That Easter-time! that Easter-time!
  But still the pure white lilies blow,
    At happy Easter-time;

And still each flower seems to say,
All people bless this holy day,
For Christ is risen, the angels say,
This blessed Easter day, this blessed Easter day.

Words used by arrangement with author, owner of the copyright.

---

**174.**

"Christ the Lord is risen to-day,"
Sons of men and angels say:
Raise your joys and triumphs high;
Sing, ye heavens, and earth, reply.

Love's redeeming work is done,
Fought the fight, the victory won;
Jesus' agony is o'er:
Darkness veils the earth no more.

Vain the stone, the watch, the seal;
Christ has burst the gates of hell:
Death in vain forbids Him rise,
Christ has opened Paradise.

Soar we now where Christ has led,
Following our exalted Head;
Made like Him, like Him we rise;
Ours the cross, the grave, the skies.

---

**175.**

Our Lord is risen from the dead,
    Our Jesus is gone up on high;
The pow'rs of hell are captive led,
    Dragged to the portals of the sky.

There His triumphal chariot waits,
   And angels chant the solemn lay,
"Lift up your heads, ye heavenly gates!
   Ye everlasting doors, give way."

Loose all your bars of massy light,
   And wide unfold the radiant scene!
He claims these mansions as His right;
   Receive the King of Glory in.

Who is the King of Glory? Who?
   The Lord, that all His foes o'ercame,
The world, sin, death and hell o'erthrew;
   And Jesus is the Conqueror's name.

---

**176.**
On this glad triumphant morning,
   Christ, the Prince of life arose;
Then the seal of death was broken,
   Now the grave with promise glows;
Mighty victor, mighty victor,
   Victor over all our foes.

CHORUS:—
   Honor, power, blessing,
Shall this mighty monarch claim;
Hallelujahs render to the Saviour's name.

When His fond, His true disciples
    To His sacred tomb drew near,
Angels from the courts of heaven
    Break the tidings full of cheer,
He is risen! He is risen!
    Christ is risen, do not fear.

Hail, all hail, triumphant hour,
    Let our happy voices say,
Christ has triumphed, man shall triumph,
    Death has lost his fearful sway;
Praise Him, praise Him, praise the Saviour
    Praise the risen Lord to-day.

---

**177.**

LET ev'ry childish voice,
    Join in a glorious song;
Let ev'ry heart rejoice,
    Let ev'ry youthful tongue
Sing to the risen Lord,
    On this glad Easter day,
In tones of reverence, the song
    Hallelujah!

Jesus, our Lord and King,
    Unto Thy loving care,
Do we our burdens bring,
    Which Thou hast died to bear;
And to the risen Lord,
    On this glad Easter day,
In tones of reverence, we'll sing
    Hallelujah!

## 178.

Low in the grave He lay—
  Jesus, my Saviour!
Waiting the coming day—
  Jesus, my Lord!

CHORUS:—(Faster.)
Up from the grave He arose,
With a mighty triumph o'er His foes;
He arose a Victor from the dark domain,
And He lives forever with His saints to reign;
He arose! He arose!
Hallelujah! Christ arose!

  Vainly they watch His bed—
    Jesus, my Saviour!
  Vainly they seal the dead—
    Jesus, my Lord!

  Death cannot keep his prey—
    Jesus, my Saviour!
  He tore the bars away—
    Jesus, my Lord!

Copyright, 1874, by Biglow & Main, used by permission.

---

## 179.

Now the bursting Spring awakes,
  Now the flowers bloom,
Now the sleeping insects creep,
  From their wint'ry tomb.

CHO.—Ring the bells! Ring the bells!
  Easter day! happy day!
Ring the bells! Ring the bells!
  Blessed Easter day!

Now the birds are flying home,
    Singing as they come;
Now the world is full of joy,
    Spring, bright Spring has come!

All ye little children dear,
    Christ is risen to-day,
And the light of His great love,
    Makes all bright and gay.

Christ, the Lord, arose this day,
    Precious souls to save;
Shout aloud, to all the world,
    His victory o'er the grave.

Used by arrangement with Oliver Ditson Co., owners of the copyright.

## 180.

Lift up, O little children,
Your voices clear and sweet,
And sing the blessed story
Of Christ, the Lord of glory,
And worship at His feet,
And worship at His feet.

Chorus:—Oh, sing the blessed story!
The Lord of life and glory
Is risen, as He said,
Is risen from the dead!

Lift up, O tender lilies,
Your whiteness to the sun;
The earth is not our prison,
Since Christ Himself hath risen,
The life of ev'ry one,
The life of ev'ry one.

Ring, all ye bells of Easter,
Your chimes of joy again,
Ring out the night of sadness,
Ring in the morn of gladness,
For death no more shall reign,
For death no more shall reign.

Copyright, 1883, by Biglow & Main, used by permission.

**181.**

The bells are merrily ringing,
And all the earth is gay;
The children joyfully singing
That Christ is risen to-day!
The earth has burst its wintry gloom,
To hail our heavenly King,
And Easter chimes, amid the gloom,
The glorious tidings bring.

How sweet they echo the story,
Those Easter chimes so gay;
All robed in heavenly glory,
Our Lord is risen to-day!
They bid each heart with joy to bloom;
The night of sorrow hath waned;
O'er all the terrors of the tomb
Our Lord hath victory gained.

We'll swell the beautiful chorus
That greets the earth so gay;
The light of heaven is o'er us,
And Christ is risen to-day!
And while our hearts with joy rebound,
We all will gratefully sing;
While merry Easter chimes resound,
To God our heavenly King.

Used by arrangement with W. A. Pond Co., owners of the copyright.

**182.**

    Snowdrops lift your timid heads,
      All the earth is waking;
    Field and forest brown and dead,
      Into life are waking.

Cho.—Snowdrops rise and tell the story,
      How He rose the Lord of glory,
    Snowdrops rise and tell the story,
      How He rose the Lord of glory.

    Lilies! lilies! Easter calls!
      Rise to meet the dawning
    Of the blessed light that falls
      Through the Easter morning.

Cho.—Ring your bells and tell the story,
      How He rose the Lord of glory,
    Ring your bells and tell the story,
      How He rose the Lord of glory.

    Waken, sleeping butterflies,
      Burst your narrow prison;
    Spread your golden wings and rise,
      For the Lord is risen.

Cho.—Spread your wings and tell the story,
      How He rose the Lord of glory,
    Spread your wings and tell the story,
      How He rose the Lord of glory.

Copyright, 1883, by Biglow & Main, used by permission.

**183.**
Sweet Easter bells are ringing,
　　Glad news their music tells;
To earth and heaven proclaiming,
　　That Christ on high now dwells.
All heaven sings forth in chorus,
　　Lift up ye gates—unfold;
Lo! here is He victorious,
　　The risen Christ foretold.

Cho.—Sweet Easter bells are ringing,
　　Glad news their music tells;
To earth and heaven proclaiming,
　　That Christ on high now dwells.

At early gray of morning,
　　In quiet hush of dawn,
Came Mary to Him weeping,
　　To find her Master gone.
For yet she knew not Jesus
　　Must rise from death again,
Or that from heaven to save us
　　He came to dwell with men.

But as she turned and saw Him,
　　Her Master and her Lord;
Sweet angel's sang a new hymn,
　　'Twas Easter's first grand chord.
And now, ye bells, keep ringing
　　Your silvery chimes ring on,
Your news to earth is bringing,
　　Glad peace to hearts forlorn.

**184.**

    From the cross on Calvary's mountain,
        Tenderly to Joseph's grave;
    Brought was Jesus slain for sinners,
        Crucified, our souls to save;
    To redeem the world from darkness,
        Cheerfully His life He gave.

    On a calm and lovely morning,
        Heaven's bright angel did appear,
    To the weeping Mary, saying,
        He is risen, He is not here;
    Go, and tell His loved disciples,
        Spread the tidings of good cheer.

    He is risen—the children's Saviour,
        Let us all in sweet accord,
    Praise Him for redemption's story,
        He has given us in His word;
    Hallelujah! hallelujah!
        Glory to the risen Lord!

---

**185.**

    Mary to her Saviour's tomb
        Hasted at the early dawn;
    Spice she brought, and sweet perfume,
        But the Lord she loved had gone:
    For awhile she weeping stood,
        Struck with sorrow and surprise,
    Shedding tears, a plenteous flood,
        For her heart supplied her eyes.

Jesus, who is always near,
   Though too often unperceived,
Came, His drooping child to cheer,
   Kindly asking why she grieved:
Though at first she knew Him not,
   When He called her by her name
Then her griefs were all forgot,
   For she found He was the same.

Grief and sighing quickly fled
   When she heard His welcome voice:
Just before, she thought Him dead,
   Now, He bids her heart rejoice;
What a change His word can make,
   Turning darkness into day!
You who weep for Jesus' sake,
   He will wipe your tears away.

---

**186.**
"I know that my Redeemer lives,"
What comfort this sweet sentence gives!
He lives, He lives, who once was dead,
He lives, my ever living Head.

He lives, to bless me with His love,
He lives, to plead for me above;
He lives, my hungry soul to feed,
He lives, to help in time of need.

He lives, to silence all my fears,
He lives, to wipe away my tears;
He lives, to calm my troubled heart
He lives, all blessings to impart.

He lives, all glory to His name!
He lives, my Jesus, still the same;
Oh, the sweet joy this sentence gives,
"I know that my Redeemer lives."]

**187.**

CHILDREN, to the risen Saviour,
  Sing aloud your praise to-day;
Praise Him for the life He gave us,
  All our debt of sin to pay.

CHO:—Hallelujah, shout His praises!
  Sing His victory o'er the grave;
Praise Him for redemption's story,
  For His wondrous power to save.

When we read the holy gospel,
  Of His suffering for our sin,
Can we not with thankful spirit,
  A new life in Him begin?

'Tis but little that He asks us,
  And His promise is sweet rest;
If we love Him, we shall meet Him,
  In the mansions of the blest.

**188.**

ALL the bells are sweet with music,
  Pealing forth their anthem free;
Christ has triumphed o'er the grave, yes,
  He has won the victory.

CHORUS:—
Ring the joyful bells at Easter,
  Sun, send out your brightest rays;
Christ is risen, o'er sin triumphant,
  Give to Him eternal praise.

Oh, to catch the mellow sweetness!
  The glad message that they ring;
Filling all our hearts completely,
  Christ is risen, our Lord and King.

Sing with joyful, happy voices,
  Christ the Lord is risen to-day!
Turn from sin, thy heart illumine,
  Walk with Him through all life's way.

---

**189.**

1 LITTLE hands are clapping now,
    Oh, how glad are we!
  In our pleasant Sabbath school
    Friends and flow'rs to see;
2 Little eyes are lifted now
    Up above the sky;
  While our voices join to sing
    3 Praise to God on high.

4 Little hands are folded now
    5 Gently on our breast;
  Thus our Shepherd takes us all
    In His arms to rest;
6 Little heads are bending now,
    Bending while we pray;
7 Asking God to fill our hearts
    With His love to-day.

8 Little eyes must read His word,
    9 Ears must hear His truth;
10 Willing feet must follow Him
    In the morn of youth;

> <sup>11</sup> Cheerful givers we must be,
> He has told us so;
> <sup>12</sup> But the gift the right hand holds,
> <sup>13</sup> Left hand must not know.

MOTIONS.—1. Clap hands. 2. Raise the eyes upward. 3. Point upward. 4. Fold hands. 5. Cross on breast. 6. Bend the head. 7. Hand on heart. 8. Hold hands as though holding an open book. 9. Touch ears. 10. Point to feet. 11. Hold out both hands. 12. Still holding out right hand. 13. Place left hand behind the back.

Copyright, 1888, by Biglow & Main, used by permission.

---

## 190.

> THE snow comes down so pure and white,
> *(Wave the hands gently.)*
> Soft and light and gentle;
> 'Tis God's message from the sky,
> Therefore, little children, try,—
> If in anger you reply,
> Remember the soft answer.

(*Repeat.*)—" A soft answer turneth away wrath: but grevious words stir up anger."—PROV. 15 : 1.

(*Sing.*)
> The rain comes pattering down so fast,
> *(Move the hand quickly up and down.)*
> Quickly, quickly falling;
> Thus God sends the welcome rain
> To freshen the flowers and fields of grain,
> All nature may drink from the fount again,
> And thirsty creatures praise Him.

(*Repeat.*)—" Whosoever will, let him take of the water of life freely."—REV. 22 : 17.

(*Sing.*)
　　After the darksome cloud has passed,
　　　(Spread the hands out before the face.)
　　Like a gloomy curtain;
　Then the sunshine's coming light,
　Like God's smile, makes all things bright,
　'Tis His love that cheers the night,
　　And rests the weary-hearted.

(*Repeat.*)—" Be of good courage, and he shall strengthen your heart, all ye that hope in the Lord."—PSALM 31 : 24.

(*Sing.*)
　　And then the rainbow of the Lord,
　　　(Raise both hands and form an arch over the head.)
　　Like a promised token;
　Brightens all the world anew,—
　'Tis His promise shining through;
　Showing us in sign so true,
　　Our Father's loving mercy.

(*Repeat.*)—" And *there was* a rainbow round about the throne."—REV. 4 : 3.

(*Sing.*)
　　Thus all the works of God, the Lord,
　　　(Spread the hands.)
　　Are so great and glorious;
　Heaven and earth shall sing in praise,
　Of His great and perfect ways;
　Till in heaven at last we gaze
　　　(Raise both hands and look up.)
　　Upon the King eternal.

(*Repeat.*)—" Thine eyes shall see the King in his beauty: they shall behold the land that is very far off."—Isa. 33: 17.

*( If preferred, a few children might stand in front of the school, and after each verse is sung, repeat the accompanying text.)
Copyright, 1896, by E. Revere.

**191.**

Little drops of water,
  Little grains of sand,
Make the mighty ocean
  ‖: And the beauteous land. :‖

And the little moments,
  Humble though they be,
Make the mighty ages
  ‖: Of eternity. :‖

So our little errors
  Lead the soul away
From the paths of virtue,
  ‖: Oft in sin to stray. :‖

Little deeds of kindness,
  Little words of love,
Make our earth an Eden
  ‖: Like the heaven above. :‖

Little seeds of mercy,
  Sown by youthful hands,
Grow to bless the nations
  ‖: Far in heathen lands. :‖

## 192.

¹ Oh, how brightly, how brightly, the *Sun* moves along,
   From the East to the West through the sky,
² Oh, how lovely, how lovely, the *Moon* looks among
   ³ All those stars as they sparkle on high.

These glorious lights the Lord hath given
⁴ To raise our thoughts from earth to heaven;
Oh, how brightly, how brightly He moves them along,
⁵ Shedding light o'er the world from on high.

MOTIONS.—1. Raise right hand and move it along. 2. Raise left hand. 3. Raise both hands and move the fingers. 4. Raise both hands. 5. Spread both hands.

---

## 193.

¹ We'll all rise up together,
² We'll all sit down together;
   We'll mind the rule in Sabbath-school,
³ And all rise up together.

⁴ We'll raise our hands together,
⁵ We'll fold our arms together;
   We'll mind the rule in Sabbath-school,
⁶ And all sit down together.

⁷ We'll turn our heads together,
⁸ We'll bend our heads together;
   We'll mind the rule in Sabbath-school,
   And all sit still together.

We'll all love one another,
Our sister and our brother;
We'll mind God's rules in Sabbath-school,
And all love one another.

Motions.—1. All rise. 2. All sit down. 3. All rise. 4. Raise hands. 5. Fold arms. 6. Sit down. 7. Turn heads from side to side. 8. Bend heads back and forth.

---

## 194.

Two little eyes to look to God,
  (Look up.)
Two little ears to hear His word,
  (Touch ears.)
Two little feet to walk in His ways,
  (Point to feet.)
Two little hands to work for Him all my days.
  (Hold out hands.)

One little tongue to speak His truth,
  (Point to tongue.)
One heart to give Him now in my youth,
  (Hand on heart.)
Take them, dear Jesus, and let them be,
Always obedient, and true to Thee.
  (Hold up hands.)

---

## 195.

I asked the little joyous bird,
  1 Who taught him how to fly,
And sing such pretty little songs,
  In the bright morning sky?
2 He told me it was God
  Who had given to him his wing,
3 And taught him how to build his nest,
  And taught him how to sing.

I asked the little lovely flower,
   ⁴ Who gave her perfume sweet,
And dressed her in her velvet coat,
   ⁵ So beautiful and neat?
⁶ She told me it was God
   Who had clothed her with such care,
⁷ And taught her how to breathe so sweet
   Upon the evening air.

⁸ I asked the little twinkling star,
   Who taught him how to shine,
And run with such a steady pace
   Along his proper line?
⁹ He told me it was God
   Who had bid him shine so bright,
¹⁰ And trim his little tiny lamp,
   To cheer the winter night.

¹¹ Since all things then, look up to God,
   The flower, the star, the bird,
And all obey His holy laws,
   ¹² And listen to His word;
¹³ I too, although a child, will try
   His bidding to obey;
That I may learn to please Him, too,
   And serve as well as they.

Words used by arrangement with Oliver Ditson Co., owners of copyright.

MOTIONS.—1. Imitate the flapping of wings. 2. Point upward. 3. Hold the hands together in form of a nest. 4. Imitate inhaling the perfume of a flower. 5. Pass both hands down on the clothes, as though smoothing them. 6. Point upward. 7. Pass the hand back and forth from the mouth, as though breathing. 8. Raise both hands, imitate the twinkling by moving the fingers. 9. Point upward. 10. Hold left hand as a lamp, with right hand imitate trimming the lamp. 11. Look up. 12. Point to the ear. 13. Point to the breast.

## 196.

Come, let us join our cheerful songs
    With angels round the throne;
Ten thousand thousand are their tongues,
    But all their joys are one.

Worthy the Lamb that died, they cry,
    To be exalted thus;
Worthy the Lamb, our lips reply,
    For He was slain for us.

Jesus is worthy to receive
    Honor and power divine;
And blessings more than we can give
    Be, Lord, forever thine.

Let all that dwell above the sky,
    And air, and earth, and seas;
Conspire to lift Thy glories high,
    And speak Thine endless praise.

---

## 197.

1 God made the sky that looks so blue,
    2 He made the grass so green;
3 He made the flowers that smell so sweet,
    In pretty colors seen.
4 God made the sun that shines so bright,
    5 And gladdens all I see;
It comes to give us heat and light,
    6 How thankful should we be!

⁷ God made the pretty bird to fly,
    How sweetly has she sung!
⁸ And though she flies so very high,
    She won't forget her young.
⁹ God made the water for my drink,
    ¹⁰ He made the fish to swim,
    He made the trees to bear nice fruit,
    ¹¹ Oh, how should I love Him!

MOTIONS.—1. Raise both hands. 2. Point down with both hands. 3. Imitate smelling flowers. 4. Spread right hand. 5. Spread both hands. 6. Cross hands on breast. 7. Imitate flying by waving both hands. 8. Raise the hands still waving, then lower them. 9. Wave hands like moving water. 10. Turn hands, and imitate fish swimming. 11. Cross hands on breast, and look up.

---

## 198.

OH, tell us how our bread is made,
    Bread is made, bread is made;
Oh, tell us how our bread is made,
    That we eat ev'ry morning.

¹ The farmer comes and sows the seed,
    Sows the seed, sows the seed;
² With harrow then he covers the seed,
    Both afternoon and morning.

³ Our Father makes the rain come down,
    Rain come down, rain come down;
⁴ He makes the glorious sun to shine,
    Both afternoon and morning.

⁵ Spring is come and the grain is up,
⁶ Grain is up, grain is up;
    Summer comes and the grain grows up
    Both afternoon and morning.

7 The reapers come and cut the grain,
    Cut the grain, cut the grain;
8 They bind it up and sing harvest home,
    Both afternoon and morning.

9 The thrashers come and beat the grain,
    Beat the grain, beat the grain;
10 With fan in hand they clean the grain,
    Both afternoon and morning.

11 The water turns and the mill goes round,
    Mill goes round, mill goes round;
And soon the rye and wheat are ground,
    Both afternoon and morning.

12 The flour and yeast are kneaded well,
    Kneaded well, kneaded well;
13 Then in the oven we bake it well,
    Both afternoon and morning.

14 We thank Thee, Lord, for this good food,
    This good food, this good food;
15 And pray to Him to make us good,
    Both afternoon and morning.

MOTIONS.—1. Imitate sowing seed with right hand. 2. With right hand make a smoothing motion. 3. Raise and lower hands rapidly, imitating falling rain. 4. Raise and move the right hand for the sun shining. 5. With both hands show how the grain peeps above the ground. 6. Raise the hands to show how the grain grows up. 7. With right hand imitate the cutting of the grain. 8. Imitate the binding up, then cross the hands on the breast. 9. With right hand imitate the beating of the grain. 10. With a fanning motion imitate the cleansing of the grain. 11. Turn right hand to imitate a wheel turning. 12. With both hands imitate the kneading of flour. 13. With both hands imitate the placing of the pan of bread in the oven. 14. Raise right hand. 15. Place hands together in the attitude of prayer and look up.

## 199.

¹ I AM so young, O Jesus,
   I do not understand
The way my soul must journey
   ² To reach the better land.
³ Oh, tell me how to love Thee,
   And what my "faith" must be:
⁴ Dear, gentle, patient teacher,
   ⁵ Explain it all to me.

⁶ Is it to trust Thy promise,
   ⁷ And simply to believe,
Like trusting in my mother,
   Whose love I would not grieve?
Her word is very precious,
   ⁸ And all in all to me;
Is this the "faith," dear Saviour,
   ⁹ That I may bring to Thee?

Thou lovest little children,
   ¹⁰ May I that love receive?
I long to be Thy dear one,
   ¹¹ Wilt Thou my sin forgive?
¹² I seem to hear a whisper,
   "Yes, darling, come to Me."
¹³ Reach down Thy hand, dear Jesus,
   ¹⁴ And draw me close to Thee.

MOTIONS.—1. Spread the hands. 2. Raise both hands. 3. Right hand on the heart. 4. Hands together as in prayer. 5. Hands clasped. 6. Finger on the lips. 7. Hand on the heart. 8. Hands crossed on breast. 9 Hands spread upward. 10. Hands spread out. 11. Hands on breast. 12. Sung in low voice, with finger raised. 13. Right hand raised toward heaven. 14. Hands crossed on breast.

Copyright, 1883, by Biglow & Main, used by permission.

## 200.

Have a clock dial. At each question move the hand to the hour mentioned. The children repeat the answer.

TEACHER.—(*Moving hand to* 1.) What says the clock when it strikes one?

SCHOOL.—Watch, says the clock, oh watch, little one.

TEACHER.—What says the clock when it strikes two?

SCHOOL.—Love God, little darling, for God loves you.

TEACHER.—Tell me now softly, what it whispers at three?

SCHOOL.—(*In whisper.*) Suffer little children to come unto me.

TEACHER.—What says the Good Shepherd, when the clock is at four?

SCHOOL.—Come, gentle lambs, come and wander no more.

TEACHER.—What is the word, when the clock is at five?

SCHOOL.—To enter the straight gate, we surely must strive.

TEACHER.—What says it at six, at the close of the day?

SCHOOL.—Our life is so short, 'twill soon pass away.

TEACHER.—What is the message when the clock is at seven?

SCHOOL.—Little children may enter the kingdom of heaven.

TEACHER.—What is the warning when the clock is at eight?

SCHOOL.—Seek Jesus early, before 'tis too late.

TEACHER.—And louder still louder, what says it at nine?

SCHOOL.—Give me my son, that proud heart of thine.

TEACHER.—What sweet song of praise, shall we echo at ten?

SCHOOL.—Hosanna in the highest, hosanna, Amen.

TEACHER.—What chorus of praise, shall we sing at eleven?

SCHOOL.—Praise be to the Father, the Father in heaven.

TEACHER.—And last of the hours, what says it at twelve?

### SCHOOL ALL RISE AND REPEAT TOGETHER.

'Tis the hour of midnight,
From darkness arise;
And haste thee, O sinner,
Oh, haste to be wise.

## CLOSING RECITATION.

### WITH CLASPED HANDS.

As the hours pass swiftly by,
Help us, Lord, to look to Thee;
So that we our days may spend
In serving Thee, the children's Friend.

**201.**

Lord, teach a little child to pray,
   (Hands together in the attitude of prayer.)
Give me the words I ought to say;
   (Touch the lips with the hand.)
For I am young, and very weak,
And know not how I ought to speak.

The words of prayer, I've often said
   (Touch lips with right hand.)
With eyelids closed and bowed head,
   (Hands on the eyes, head bowed.)
But, oh, I'm very much afraid
That with my heart I've never prayed.
   (Right hand on heart.)

But now, O God, be pleased to take
Away this heart, for Jesus' sake;
   (Wave the hand away from heart.)
Oh, give me one that loves to pray,
   (Hands together in the attitude of prayer.)
And read the Bible every day.

---

**202.**

1 Little gentle breath,
   Coming and going away
Who keeps you coming, coming
   By night as well as by day?

2 Little busy heart,
   3 Beating, beating away,
Who keeps you beating, beating
   By night as well as by day?

4 God moves each busy heart,
   5 God sends each gentle breath;
6 God watches us night and day,
   7 And keeps us safe from death.

⁸ Little merry child,
⁹ Sporting, sporting away,
¹⁰ God keeps you living, breathing,
By night as well as by day.

MOTIONS.—1. Move the hand back and forth from the mouth. 2. Lay right hand on the heart. 3. Make a patting motion with the hands on the heart to imitate its beating. 4. Raise right hand and point upward. 5. Point to the mouth. 6. Raise both hands. 7. Fold the arms together. 8. Spread out the hands. 9. Wave the hands. 10. Right hand moving back and forth from the mouth.

Copyright, 1875, by Biglow & Main, used by permission.

---

## 203.

THE Lord has made me, yet sometimes,
  (Point upward.)
I greatly wonder why,
He should have formed with wondrous skill,
  So small a child as I.
  (Hands on shoulders.)

My head, so filled with wondrous thoughts
  (Point to the head.)
My eye so quick and keen,
  (Point to the eye.)
My listening ear, my speaking tongue;
  (Point to the ear.)    (Point to mouth.)
  How marvelous they seem!

My *hand* so curiously made
  (Hold out the hand.)
  That I can move at will;
  (Move hand back and forth.)
My agile *limbs*, my nimble *feet*,
  (Move feet alternately.)
  Are wonders, wonders still.

The *pulses* quick that *beat* and *beat*,
(Place right finger on left wrist, mark the beats of the pulse with finger.)
   And never, never rest;
My heart, that little life clock there
   (Hand on heart.)
   That ticketh in my breast.
(Move hand up and down—like the beating of heart.)

O what am I, that God the Lord
   (Raise hand.)
   Should form a child like me;
   (Hand on breast.)
So humble in my low estate,
   So great and glorious He.
   (Both hands raised.)

Let me devote my life to Thee,
   (Hand on breast.)
   My Maker and my God
Oh, take me, make me Thine own child,
   (Hold out both hands.)
   Through Jesus Christ our Lord.

---

**204.**
1 I'VE two little hands to work for Jesus,
  2 One little tongue His praise to tell;
3 Two little ears to hear His counsel,
  4 One little voice a song to swell.

CHORUS:—
  9 Lord we come, Lord we come,
    In our childhood's early morning,
  10 Lord we come, Lord we come,
    Come to learn of Thee.

⁵ I've two little feet to tread the pathway
⁶ Up to the heavenly courts above;
⁷ Two little eyes to read the Bible,
   Telling of Jesus' wond'rous love.

⁸ I've one little heart to give to Jesus,
   One little soul for Him to save;
 One little life for His dear service,
   One little self that He must have.

MOTIONS.—1. Hold out hands. 2. Point to tongue. 3. Touch the ears 4. Point to mouth. 5. Point to feet. 6. Point up. 7. Touch eyes. 8. Hand on heart. 9. Spread hands. 10. Spread hands.

Used by permission of D. C. Cook Publishing Co., owners of the copyright.

---

## 205.

LITTLE knees should lowly bend
          (Kneel with clasped hands.)
   At the time of prayer;
Little thoughts to heaven ascend
          (Point to heaven, and rise.)
   To our Father there.

Little hands should usefully
          (Hands spread.)
   In employment move;
Little feet should cheerfully
          (Point to the feet.)
   Run on works of love.

Little tongues should speak the truth,
          (Point to the tongue.)
   As by Scripture taught;
Little lips should ne'er be loth
          (Point to the lips.)
   To confess a fault.

Little ears should listen to
      (Point to the ears.)
 All the Bible says;
Little bosoms throb to do
      (Cross hands on bosom.)
 What the Lord will please.

Little spirits should be glad
 Jesus died to save;
      (Spread out the hands.)
Oh, how cold and dark and sad
 Else would be the grave!

Little children sinners are;
 But the Saviour says
All that seek Him now by prayer
  (Bow the head and clasp hands together.)
 Shall obtain His grace.

Little infants dying go
      (Raise the hands.)
 To the world above;
And our souls shall join them too,
  (Clasp hands over the breast, and look up.)
 If we Jesus love.

---

**206.**

1 WE'LL all stand up together,
 2 And ask God's blessing here;
To rest on ev'ry scholar,
 And on our teacher dear.

3 Oh take our hearts, dear Saviour,
 And wash them with Thy blood;
Help us, as we walk through life,
 4 To keep God's holy word.

5 Dear Father, take our bodies
  And keep them undefiled;
6 In praise let us sing to Thee,
  7 For Thou dost love each child.

8 We'll look straight at our teacher,
  And help her all we can;
  By learning well the precious word
  9 That God has given to man.

10 Now we will all be seated,
  11 Our hands together fold;
  We'll all try to remember,
  To do as we are told.

MOTIONS—1. Rise. 2. Hands as in prayer. 3. Hand on heart. 4. Point up. 5. Hands on chest. 6. Point up. 7. Hand on chest. 8. Look at teacher. 9. Point up. 10. Sit down. 11. Fold hands.

---

## 207.

1 RISE up, rise up so promptly,
  Rise up, rise up so promptly,
  Rise up, rise up so promptly,
2 And fold your arms like me, like me.

3 Wave your hands, wave your hands so gently, etc.
4 And fold your arms like me, like me.

5 Clap your hands, clap your hands so brightly, etc.
6 And fold your arms like me, like me.

7 Roll your hands, roll your hands so softly, etc.
8 And fold your arms like me, like me.

⁹ Sit down, sit down so quietly, etc.
¹⁰ And fold your arms like me, like me.

¹¹ Do not speak, do not speak in schooltime, etc.
¹² And fold your arms like me, like me.

MOTIONS.—1. Rise. 2. Fold arms. 3. Wave hands. 4. Fold arms. 5. Clap hands. 6. Fold arms. 7. Roll hands. 8. Fold arms. 9. Sit down. 10. Fold arms. 11. Point to the lips. 12. Fold arms.

---

## 208.

1.—" He shall build a house for my name."—2 SAM. 7 : 13.

2.—" Therefore now let it please thee to bless the house of thy servant, . . . and with thy blessing let the house of thy servant be blessed forever."—2 SAM. 7 : 29.

(Here place the foundation.)

3.—" The foundation of the house of the Lord was laid."—EZRA 3 : 11.

4.—" For other foundation can no man lay than that is laid, which is Jesus Christ."—1 COR. 3 : 11.

5.—" Jesus Christ himself being the chief corner *stone.*"—EPH. 2 : 20.

(Here build the walls.)

6.—" Do good in thy good pleasure unto Zion : build thou the walls of Jerusalem."—Ps. 51 : 18.

(Here place the door.)

7.—" I am the door : by me if any man enter in, he shall be saved."—JOHN 10 : 9.

8.—" Enter into his gates with thanksgiving, *and* into his courts with praise."—Ps. 100:4.

(Here place the pillars.)

9.—" And he reared up the pillars before the temple, one on the right hand and the other on the left."—2 CHRON. 3:17.

10.—" Him that overcometh will I make a pillar in the temple of my God."—REV. 3:12.

11.—" I had rather be a doorkeeper in the house of my God, than to dwell in the tents of wickedness."—Ps. 84:10.

(Here place the tower.)

12.—" The name of the Lord is a strong tower; the righteous runneth into it, and is safe."—PROV. 18:10.

13.—" Looking unto Jesus the author and finisher of *our* faith; who ... is set down at the right hand of the throne of God."—HEBREW 12:2.

\* (Have a miniature church, to be put together in parts; the texts are to be repeated as each part is laid.)

(*Sing the hymn at the close of the building.*)

---

## 209.

THE church of God through ages past,
   Has grown by work and prayer,
And children should not be the last
   To take their offerings there.
Though small "church builders" few and weak,
   Our efforts may be seen,
By here a brick and there a brick,
   With earnest prayers between.

God never calls a child to do
   The work He gives a man;
He says, My grace will see you through,
   If you do what you can.
So, step by step, the church of God
   Will rise to heights serene,
If here a brick and there a brick,
   With earnest prayers between.

But we, ourselves, are temples too,
   Wherein God's spirit dwells;
So lay foundations firm and true,
   Just as the Bible tells.
God's measuring rod of righteousness
   Will make the walls four-square,
Then here a brick and there a brick,
   And in between, a prayer.

## 210.

1 'Tis in the Bible that we read,
A sower went forth to sow his seed;
He flung it broadcast over the land
With liberal heart and open hand.

CHORUS:—

We are sowing the gospel seed,
   (Imitate sowing seed.)
On which the hungry soul may feed!
Let us do it with cheerful hand,
We little lambs of Jesus' band.

2 And as he sowed some fell by the way
3 On the hard, cold ground and there it lay;
4 The people trod it under their feet,
5 And birds of the air, the seed did eat.

⁶ Some seed on stony ground was flung,
⁷ And very soon it upward sprung;
  So little earth was where it lay
⁸ That, when the sun rose, it withered away.

  Some seed among the thorns did fall,
⁹ Which grew up too, and choked it all;
  No truth with God will e'er be found,
  When thorns and weeds infest the ground.

  And other seed on good ground fell,
¹⁰ The sun and rain, the seed did swell;
¹¹ Firm rooted too, first blade, then ear,
  A hundredfold for God did bear.

¹² Now, let each one that hath an ear,
  Lend it to Christ, and for Him hear—
¹³ In each heart may God's word take root,
¹⁴ Tongue, ¹⁵ hands and ¹⁶ feet, for Him bear fruit.

MOTIONS.—1. Imitate the sowing of seed. 2. Sow seed. 3. Point to ground. 4. Move feet up and down. 5. Spread the hands like wings. 6. Sow seed. 7. Raise the hands. 8. Raise the hands with fingers touching, and spread apart over the head. 9. Clasp the hands one over the other. 10. Raise the hands, then lower for the rain. 11. Begin low with one finger then hands—then raise both hands. 12. Point to the ear. 13. Hand over heart and point above. 14. Point to tongue. 15. Spread hands. 16. Point to feet.

---

**211.**
  BEGIN the day with God,
         (Kneel.)
  Kneel down to Him in prayer;
  Lift up thy heart to His abode,
  And seek His love to share.

Open the Book of God
   (Spread the hands like an open book.)
 And read a portion there,
That it may hallow all thy thoughts,
 And sweeten all thy care.


Go through the day with God:
    (Cross hands on bosom.)
 Whate'er thy work may be;
Where'er thou art, at home, abroad,
 He still is near to thee.


Conclude the day with God:
    (Clasp hands as in prayer.)
 Thy sins to Him confess;
Trust in the Lord's atoning blood
 And plead His righteousness.


Lie down at night with God,
  (Lean head on hand and close the eyes.)
 Who gives His servants sleep;
And when thou tread'st the vale of death
 He will thee guard and keep.
    (Clasp hands on the heart.)


"My voice shall Thou hear in the morning, O Lord; in the morning will I direct my prayer unto Thee and will look up."—Ps. 5 : 3.
   (Look up.)

"Commit thy way unto the Lord; trust also in Him; and He shall bring *it* to pass."—Ps. 37 : 5.
 (Spread hands toward God, then clasp hands.)

## 212.

1. Lift up your hands in the sanctuary and bless the Lord.
   (Hands raised.)
2. O clap your hands, all ye people.
   (Clap hands.)
3. Thy word have I hid in mine heart.
   (Cross hands on breast.)
4. Stand up and bless the Lord.
   (Rise.)
5. His banner over us is love.
   (Join tips of fingers over the head.)
6. Happy is the man that findeth wisdom.
   (Hands at the side.)
7. Length of days is in her right hand.
   (Right hand extended.)
8. And in her left hand riches and honor.
   (Left hand extended.)
9. Her ways are ways of pleasantness, and all her paths are peace.
   (Clap hands three times.)
10. Him that overcometh will I grant to sit with me in my throne.

---

## 213.

Brightly gleams our banner,
   Pointing to the sky,
Waving wanderers onward
   To their homes on high.
Journeying o'er the desert,
   Gladly thus we pray,
And, with hearts united,
   Take our heavenward way.

Chorus:—Brightly gleams our banner,
   Pointing to the sky,
Waving wanderers onward
   To their homes on high.

Jesus, Lord and Master,
   At thy sacred feet,
Here with hearts rejoicing
   See Thy children meet;
Often we have left Thee,
   Often gone astray;
Keep us, mighty Saviour,
   In the narrow way.

All our days direct us
   In the way we go;
Lead us on victorious
   Over ev'ry foe:
Bid Thine angels shield us
   When the storm-clouds lower,
Pardon Thou and save us
   In the last dread hour.

**214.**
Now who are these, whose little feet
   Are marching bravely on,
With faces bright, with cheerful hearts,
   And voices raised in song?
These are the children of the King,
   And walking in His way;
They're journeying in the narrow path,
   To realms of endless day.

What is the song these children sing
   With voices sweet and clear,
That gives the weary traveler hope,
   And angels bend to hear?
It is a hymn of humble praise,
   To God the Father given;
Of trust in Him who shows the road,
   That leads them on to Heaven.

Who is the Captain of this band,
    Who makes their pathway bright?
He guides their steps, He clears their way,
    And makes their burdens light.
'Tis Jesus Christ, the children's friend,
    Who saved them by his love;
He died for them that they might share
    His home in Heaven above.

---

**215.**

We are marching to the river,
    'Tis almost in sight!
With the loved and blest forever,
    We shall walk in light!
We can almost hear the flowing
    Of that rushing tide!
To the Land of love we're going,
    Where our hopes abide!

Cho.—We are marching to the river,
    'Tis almost in sight!
Just across, we'll meet the angels
    Robed in spotless white!

Loving ones will come to meet us,
    On the further shore!
Gentle voices there will greet us,
    And we'll weep no more!
Step by step, that shore we're nearing,
    And the Saviour's hand
Leads us onward, never fearing,
    To the Better Land!

Used by permission of Hamilton S. Gordon, owner of copyright.

**216.**

We are little travelers,
   Marching, marching,
We are little travelers,
   Marching on;
Walking in the narrow way,
Shunning paths that lead astray,
We are little travelers,
   Marching on.

We are little laborers,
   Working, working,
We are little laborers,
   Working on;
Never idling time away,
Busy working ev'ry day,
We are little laborers,
   Working on.

We are little soldiers,
   Fighting, fighting,
We are little soldiers,
   Fighting on;
Warring 'gainst the power of sin,
Foes without and foes within,
We are little soldiers,
   Fighting on.

We are little pilgrims,
   Hoping, hoping,
We are little pilgrims,
   Hoping on;
For a country better far,
Where our crown and kingdom are,
We are little pilgrims,
   Hoping on.

Copyright, 1873, by Biglow & Main, used by permission.

**217.**
　　　Sound the battle cry!
　　　See! the foe is nigh;
　　　Raise the standard high
　　　　　For the Lord;
　　　Gird your armor on,
　　　Stand firm ev'ry one;
　　　Rest your cause upon
　　　　　His holy word.

Chorus:—
　Rouse then, soldiers! rally round the banner!
　　Ready, steady, pass the word along;
　Onward, forward, shout aloud hosannah!
　　Christ is Captain of the mighty throng.

　　　Strong to meet the foe,
　　　Marching on we go,
　　　While our cause we know
　　　　　Must prevail;
　　　Shield and banner bright
　　　Gleaming in the light;
　　　Battling for the right
　　　　　We ne'er can fail.

　　　Oh! Thou God of all,
　　　Hear us when we call;
　　　Help us one and all
　　　　　By Thy grace;
　　　When the battle's done,
　　　And the victory won,
　　　May we wear the crown
　　　　　Before Thy face.

Copyright, 1869, by Biglow & Main, used by permission.

## 218.

I am a little soldier,
    And not yet very old;
I mean to fight for Jesus,
    And wear a crown of gold;
I know He makes me happy,
    And loves me all the day;
I'll be His little soldier,
    The Bible says I may.

I love my precious Saviour,
    Because He died for me,
And if I did not serve Him,
    How sinful I would be;
He gives me ev'ry comfort,
    And hears me when I pray;
I want to live for Jesus,
    The Bible says I may.

I now can do a little,
    But when I older grow,
I'll try to do for Jesus
    The greatest good I know;
God help and keep me faithful
    In all I do and say;
I want to live a Christian,
    The Bible says I may.

From Infant Praises by per. of John J. Hood.

## 219.

Though I am a little child,
    We never are too small
To work for Him who teaches us,
    He died to save us all;

Scholars, friends, and teachers dear,
   Serve the Lord with love and fear,
Then we'll meet to sing His praise
   In heaven, our promised home.

CHORUS:—March on, march on,
   Scholars, ev'ry one,
   Toil on, strive on,
   Till the victory's won,
   Never lay our weapons down,
   Till we've won the victor's crown,
   Then we'll meet to sing His praise
   In heaven, our promised home.

Little hearts and little hands
   May find some work to do,
Little prayers be heard in heaven,
   And answered sometimes too;
Do not be discouraged then,
   Jesus is the children's friend,
And will meet us at the gate
   Of heaven, our promised home.

Little lips may always utter
   Songs of love and praise,
Little feet may learn to tread
   The path to endless days;
Gentle Saviour hear my prayer,
   Keep my heart from ev'ry snare,
Meet us, greet us, over there,
   In heaven, our promised home.

**220.**

Keeping step with Jesus,
  Though the way be long;
We ne'er miss the pathway,
  We can ne'er go wrong.
Keeping step with Jesus,
  Straining ev'ry limb;
Onward, ever onward,
  Keeping step with Him.

Keeping step with Jesus,
  Even in the dark;
We can hear His footsteps,
  Though unseen its mark.
Though we walk in shadow,
  Treading pathways new;
Marking time with Jesus,
  Step we ever true.

Keeping step with Jesus,
  Nothing can alarm;
Foes will never hurt us,
  Naught will do us harm.
Walking close beside Him,
  His strong arm our stay;
Oh, how safe the journey
  O'er an untried way!

Keeping step with Jesus,
  Never on before;
Brighter grows the pathway,
  Shining more and more.
Till by living fountains,
  Bathed in heaven's light;
We through fields of glory
  Walk with Him in white.

**221.**

In days of old when Christ the Lord
  Among His people dwelt,
To little ones He often showed
  The love for them He felt;
Close to His side the children pressed,
  He turned away not one;
"In these, and such as these," He said,
  "My kingdom is begun."

Chorus:—

  Hosanna! hosanna!
  Hosanna in the highest!

One day unto His Father's house
  With troubled heart He came,
His hour of trial now drew near,
  And near the death of shame;
More foes than friends about Him stood,
  He heard no word of cheer,
When lo! from children's lips arose
  An anthem sweet and clear.

A smile lit up the Saviour's face,
  He called it perfect praise,
That thus on shadow of the cross,
  Threw sunny hope's bright rays;
Like children of that olden time
  We, too, hosanna sing,
For in this temple man has made,
  Waits, though unseen, our King!

**222.**

I am singing, singing,
　Singing all day long;
Through my heart is ringing
　One unceasing song.
Glory be to Jesus!
　Glory to the Lamb!
By whose blood so precious,
　Clean and whole I am.

Chorus:—I am singing, singing,
　　Singing all day long;
　Through my heart is ringing
　　One unceasing song.

When at early morning
　From my bed I spring,
When the shadowy evening
　Folds me in its wing.
While I'm at my study,
　While I'm at my play,
Sings my heart of Jesus,
　Through the livelong day.

Yes, I'll sing of Jesus,
　And His tender love;
Till I stand before Him,
　In the courts above.
Then I'll join the chorus
　Of the heavenly throng,
While the angels listen
　To the grand new song.

**223.**
Here are joyous faces,
　　Making all things gay;
Marking with our gladness,
　　This bright, happy day.
Send your voices upward,
　　Praise your gracious King;
Raise the roof with anthems,
　　Make the heavens ring.

Chorus:—(In unison.)
Bring the humblest offering,
　　Lay it at His feet;
Self and all we have for Christ,
　　Sacrifice complete.

Here we're taught the Scriptures,
　　Here we learn the way
Up to God the Father,
　　Nearer day by day.
Jesus ever faithful,
　　Tells us: Follow me,
I will lead you safely,
　　Through eternity.

---

**224.**
Lift up your faces o'er hill and vale,
　　Ye lilies in beauty waving;
Ye streams that flow, sing soft and low,
　　Your sunny flower banks laving.

Refrain:—
Let all things beautiful praise the Lord,
　　Let children's voices praise Him:
We'll join in the song of the angel throng,
　　Forever praise the Lord.

Lift up your faces o'er hill and vale,
   O'er meadows and valleys blooming;
The lilies feet are fair and sweet,
   The soft wind's breath perfuming.

Copyright, 1893, by Biglow & Main, used by permission.

---

**225.**
ON this happy day we gather,
   'Mid the sunshine and the flowers,
All around us joy and blessings,
   Fall like soft refreshing showers;
Our young hearts are full of gladness,
   Our young lips are full of praise,
We have come to thank Thee, Father,
   For the love that crowns our days.

For this Christian land we praise Thee,
   Stretching out to East and West;
For the precious open Bible,
   For the holy Sabbath rest;
And for all the many mercies
   Thou dost shower upon us here,
For the light of Thy love ever
   Bringeth us to Thee more near.

And for Jesus Christ our Saviour,
   Better than all gifts beside,
For the blessed Holy Spirit
   Sent our timid steps to guide;
Thanks for all, dear Lord, we bring Thee,
   As we gather here to-day,
And may ev'ry one departing,
   Some sweet blessings bear away.

**226.**

A LITTLE song for Jesus,
  Awake and sing, my soul,
A gladsome song for Jesus,
  Whose blood has made thee whole;
Sing of the healing fountain,
  In loud and lofty strain,
Till ev'ry listening mountain
  Shall echo the refrain.

A little song for Jesus,
  In simple words and plain,
Borne on the passing breezes,
  Some listless ear may gain;
May reach some dull soul sleeping,
  As wafted seed, the mould,
And at the time of reaping,
  May yield an hundredfold.

A little song for Jesus,
  Winged with a silent prayer,
The broken spirit eases
  Of more than half its care;
And leaden skies grow clearer,
  And lighter leans the load,
When souls are lifted nearer,
  By holy song, to God.

A little song for Jesus,
  Thy gladdest, noblest lay,
Lift up, my soul, for Jesus
  Who bore thy sins away;
Lift up o'er rock and river,
  O'er land and foaming tide,
And be the glory ever
  Unto the Christ that died.

**227.**
    Glory, glory, hallelujah!
      Thus, O Lord, to Thee we sing,
    To this temple of Thy service,
      We our loving tribute bring.

Cho.—Praise Him, praise Him, Prince of Glory!
      To Him now, our anthem sing,
    Jesus reigns, and lives forever,
      We will crown Him Lord and King.

    On this blessed, holy Sabbath,
      In Thy house, how glad are we,
    May our hearts be pure in worship,
      May we give ourselves to Thee.

    Saviour, help us, take us, keep us,
      From all sin and sorrow free,
    Fold Thy loving arms around us,
      May we Thy dear children be.

    And at last, when life is ended,
      Take us to Thy home above,
    May we dwell with Thee so happy
      In Thine everlasting love.

---

**228.**
  Jesus invites you, oh, do not delay,
  Come closer to Him, He wants you to stay;
  Though you are helpless, so weary and sad,
  Jesus will save you, and make your heart glad.

Chorus:—
  Jesus is calling, Jesus is calling,
  Don't keep Him waiting, His love is so true;
  Jesus is calling, the night is falling,
  Jesus is calling, because He loves you.

We know that Jesus is willing to bless,
All who are weary at heart, and distressed;
Keeping us ever in His gracious care,
Do not turn from Him, for He's waiting there.

How can we thank Him for all His great love?
Morning and eve let your prayers reach above;
Knowing that Jesus has said unto thee,
"Suffer the children to come unto Me."

---

**229.**

On this our glad birthday,
   Dear Jesus, we sing,
And praise Thee and bless Thee,
   Our Saviour and King;
Our gifts now we bring Thee,
   With thanks for Thy care,
And pray for Thy blessing
   Through each coming year.

Kind Shepherd, keep all in
   The fold of Thy love,
Let none of us wander,
   And from Thee remove;
May ev'ry one's birthday
   A better child see,
Who grows more and more, Lord,
   In likeness to Thee.

---

**230.**

I love to hear the story
   Which angel voices tell,
How once the King of Glory
   Came down on earth to dwell.

I am both weak and sinful,
  But this I surely know,
The Lord came down to save me,
  Because he loved me so.

I'm glad my blessed Saviour
  Was once a child like me,
To show how pure and holy
  His little ones might be;
And if I try to follow
  His footsteps here below,
He never will forget me,
  Because He loved me so.

To sing His love and mercy
  My sweetest songs I'll raise,
And though I cannot see Him,
  I know He hears my praise;
For He has kindly promised
  That I shall surely go
To sing among His angels,
  Because He loved me so.

---

## 231.

GOD be with you till we meet again!—
By His counsels guide, uphold you,
With His sheep securely fold you;
God be with you till we meet again!

CHORUS:—
  Till we meet! Till we meet!
  Till we meet at Jesus' feet;
  Till we meet! Till we meet!
  God be with you till we meet again!

God be with you till we meet again!—
'Neath His wings protecting hide you,
Daily manna still divide you;
God be with you till we meet again!

God be with you till we meet again!—
Keep love's banner floating o'er you,
Smite death's threatening wave before you;
God be with you till we meet again!

Used by arrangement with Rev. J. E. Rankin, owner of the copyright.

---

**232.**
A.—" Ask, and it shall be given you; seek, and ye shall find; knock, and it shall be opened unto you."—MATT. 7:7.

B.—" Behold the Lamb of God, which taketh away the sin of the world!"—JOHN 1:29.

C.—" Children, obey your parents in the Lord: for this is right."—EPH. 6:1.

D.—" Draw nigh to God, and he will draw nigh to you."—JAMES 4:8.

E.—" Even a child is known by his doings, whether his work *be* pure, and whether *it be* right."—PROV. 20:11.

F.—" Freely ye have received, freely give."—MATT. 10:8.

**G.**—" God so loved the world, that he gave his only begotten Son, that whosoever believeth in him should not perish, but have everlasting life."—JOHN 3: 16.

**H.**—" Him that cometh to me I will in no wise cast out."—JOHN 6: 37.

**I.**—" I will arise and go to my father, and will say unto him, Father, I have sinned against heaven, and before thee, and am no more worthy to be called thy son."—LUKE 15: 18, 19.

**J.**—" Judge not, that ye be not judged."—MATT. 7:1.

**K.**—" Keep thy heart with all diligence; for out of it *are* the issues of life.—PROV. 4: 23.

**L.**—" Lying lips *are* abomination to the Lord."—PROV. 12: 22.

**M.**—" My son, if sinners entice thee, consent thou not."—PROV. 1: 10.

**N.**—" Now *is* the accepted time; behold, now *is* the day of salvation."—2 COR. 6: 2.

**O.**—" Open thou mine eyes, that I may behold wondrous things out of thy law."—Ps. 119: 18.

**P.**—" Pray without ceasing."—1 THESS. 5: 17.

**Q.**—" Quench not the Spirit."—1 THESS. 5: 19.

R.—" Resist the devil, and he will flee from you."
—James 4 : 7.

S.—" Suffer the little children to come unto me, and forbid them not; for of such is the kingdom of God."—Mark 10 : 14.

T.—" Thou God seest me."—Gen. 16 : 13.

U.—" Unto the upright there ariseth light in the darkness."—Ps. 112 : 4.

V.—" Verily, verily, I say unto you, Whatsoever ye shall ask the Father in my name, he will give *it* you."—John 16 : 23.

W. (Golden Rule.)—" Whatsoever ye would that men should do to you, do ye even so to them."—Matt. 7 : 12.

Y.—" Ye must be born again."—John 3 : 7.

Z.—" Zion shall be redeemed with judgment, and her converts with righteousness."—Isaiah 1 : 27.

## 233.
1.—" Watch."—Mark 13 : 37.
2.—" Follow me."—John 21 : 19.
3.—" Come unto me."—Matt. 11 : 28.
4.—" Christ died for us."—Rom. 5 : 8.
5.—" Ye must be born again."—John 3 : 7.
6.—" Lo, I am with you alway."—Matt. 28 : 20.
7.—" What must I do to be saved ?"—Acts 16 : 30.

8.—"I go to prepare a place for you."—John 14 : 2.

9.—"Christ Jesus came into the world to save sinners."—1 Tim. 1 : 15.

10.—"What shall a man give in exchange for his soul."—Mark 8 : 37.

11.—"Believe on the Lord Jesus Christ, and thou shalt be saved."—Acts 16 : 31.

12.—"The blood of Jesus Christ his Son cleanseth us from all sin."—1 John 1 : 7.

---

**234.**
Abide with me: fast falls the eventide;
The darkness deepens; Lord, with me abide;
When other helpers fail, and comforts flee,
Help of the helpless, oh, abide with me.

Swift to its close ebbs out life's little day;
Earth's joys grow dim, its glories pass away,
Change and decay in all around I see;
O Thou Who changest not, abide with me.

I need Thy presence every passing hour;
What but Thy grace can foil the tempter's power?
Who like Thyself, my guide and stay can be?
Through cloud and sunshine, Lord, abide with me.

I fear no foe, with Thee at hand to bless:
Ills have no weight, and tears no bitterness.
Where is death's sting? where, grave, thy victory?
I triumph still, if Thou abide with me.

Hold Thou Thy cross before my closing eyes;
Shine through the gloom, and point me to the skies;
Heaven's morning breaks, and earth's vain shadows
    flee ;
In life, in death, O Lord, abide with me.

**235.**

We love to sing of Jesus,
    Who died our souls to save;
We love to sing of Jesus,
    Triumphant o'er the grave;
And in our hour of danger,
    We'll trust His love alone,
Who once slept in a manger,
    And now sits on the throne.

Then let us sing of Jesus,
    While yet on earth we stay,
And hope to sing of Jesus,
    Throughout eternal day;
For those who here confess Him,
    He will in heaven confess;
And faithful hearts that bless Him,
    He will forever bless.

---

**236.**

Glory to the Father give,
God, in whom we move and live;
Children's prayers He deigns to hear,
Children's songs delight His ear.
Glory to the Son we bring,
Christ, our Prophet, Priest, and King,
Children, raise your sweetest strain
To the Lamb, for He was slain.

Glory to the Holy Ghost,
He reclaims the sinner lost;
Children's minds may He inspire,
Touch their tongues with holy fire.

Glory in the highest be
To the blessed Trinity,
For the gospel from above,
For the word that "God is love."

---

**237.**

I BELIEVE in God the Father,
   Maker of heaven and earth:
The Creator, in whose image
   Man was made to rule the earth.
He made the moon, the stars, and sun
   And gave us night and day.
"Our Father, who art in heaven,"—
   'Tis thus to Him I pray.


And Jesus Christ, His only Son,
   Who, of a virgin born,
Came down to earth my life to save
   By giving up His own.
I believe in Him, my Saviour,
   My Lord, the crucified;
To take away my sins He came
   And suffered, bled and died.


I believe in the Holy Ghost—
   God's Spirit sent in love,
By whom I must be born again—
   To reach my home above.
May honor, praise and glory, rise
   From all below the sky,
To Father, Son, and Holy Ghost—
   The Triune God on high!

**238.**
    Glory, glory to the Father,
      Who, with tender care,
    Watches alway o'er His children,
      Welcoming their praise and prayer.

Cho.—Lifting up our voices,
      Lord we worship Thee,
    Father, Son, and Holy Spirit,
      Ever blessed Trinity.

    Glory, glory be to Jesus,
      Saviour, brother, friend—
    We would love and serve Thee truly,
      For the love that knows no end.

    Glory to the Holy Spirit,
      Fellowship Divine.
    Come and dwell in us, we pray Thee,
      In our hearts forever shine.

# MANUAL FOR PRIMARY SUNDAY-SCHOOLS.

## BEING

# SCRIPTURE LESSONS

## FOR YOUNG SCHOLARS.

*Hymn.*—Holy Bible, book divine. Page 5.

QUESTION 1. *What book should children study the most, and love the best?*

*Answer to Question* 1. The holy Scriptures, which are able to make thee wise unto salvation through faith which is in Christ Jesus. 2 Timothy 3:15.

Thy word have I hid in mine heart, that I might not sin against thee. Psalm 119:11.

*Hymn.*—Oh, send forth the Bible, more precious than gold! Page 108.

Q. 2. *What does the Bible tell us about God?*

A. He is wise in heart, and mighty in strength. Job 9:4.

Can any hide himself in secret places that I shall not see him? saith the Lord. Do not I fill heaven and earth? said the Lord. Jeremiah 23:24.

*Hymn.*—Almighty God, thy piercing eye. Page 84.

Q. 3. *Who made all things?*

A. In the beginning God created the heaven and the earth. Genesis 1:1.

*Hymn.*—It is God's mercy gives us. Page 11.

Q. 4. *Of what did God make man?*

A. The LORD God formed man *of* the dust of the ground, and breathed into his nostrils the breath of life; and man became a living soul. Genesis 2:7.

Q. 5. *In whose image did God make man?*

A. God created man in his own image, in the image of God created he him. Genesis 1:27.

*Hymn.*—I sing the mighty power of God. Page 11.

Q. 6. *If God created man holy, how did man become a sinner?*

A. The serpent beguiled Eve through his subtilty. 2 Corinthians 11:3.

And when the woman saw that the tree *was* good for food, and that it *was* pleasant to the eyes, and a tree to be desired to make *one* wise, she took of the fruit thereof, and did eat, and gave also unto her husband with her; and he did eat. Genesis 3:6.

By one man sin entered into the world, and death by sin; and so death passed upon all men, for that all have sinned. Romans 5:12.

*Hymn.*—Jesus, Saviour, pity me. Page 81.

Q. 7. *How did God show his love to sinful man?*

A. God so loved the world, that he gave his only begotten Son, that whosoever believeth in him should not perish, but have everlasting life. John 3:16.

*Hymn.*—How precious is the story. Page 19.

Q. 8. *Where was Jesus born?*

A. In Bethlehem of Judea, in the days of Herod the king. Matthew 2:1.

And the angel said unto them, Fear not: for, behold, I bring you good tidings of great joy, which shall be to all people. For unto you is born this day in the city of David a Saviour, which is Christ the Lord. Luke 2: 10, 11.

*Hymn.*—While shepherds watched their flocks by night. Page 129.

Q. 9. *What do we know of the childhood of Jesus?*

A. The child grew, and waxed strong in spirit, filled with wisdom; and the grace of God was upon him. Luke 2: 40.

And he went down with them, and came to Nazareth, and was subject unto them. Luke 2: 51.

And Jesus increased in wisdom and stature, and in favor with God and man. Luke 2: 52.

*Hymn.*—Jesus, when a little child. Page 44.

Q. 10. *What do we first read about Jesus after he became a man?*

A. Then cometh Jesus from Galilee to Jordan unto John, to be baptized of him. Matthew 3: 13.

And Jesus, when he was baptized, went up straightway out of the water: and, lo, the heavens were opened unto him, and he saw the Spirit of God descending like a dove, and lighting upon him:

And lo a voice from heaven, saying, This is my beloved Son, in whom I am well pleased. Matthew 3: 16, 17.

*Hymn.*—More like Jesus would I be. Page 47.

Q. 11. *What next do we read about Jesus?*

A. And immediately the Spirit driveth him into the wilderness.

And he was there in the wilderness forty days

tempted of Satan; and was with the wild beasts; and the angels ministered unto him.  Mark 1 : 12, 13.

*Hymn.*—Jesus lover of my soul.  Page 88.

**Q. 12.** *What did Jesus do for the people as he walked about among them?*

A.  Jesus went about all the cities and villages, teaching in their synagogues, and preaching the gospel of the kingdom, and healing every sickness and every disease among the people.  Matthew 9: 35.

*Hymn.*—One there is above all others.  Page 18.

**Q. 13.** *Did Jesus love children when he lived upon earth?*

A.  And they brought young children to him, that he should touch them; and *his* disciples rebuked those that brought *them*.

But when Jesus saw *it*, he was much displeased, and said unto them, Suffer the little children to come unto me, and forbid them not; for of such is the kingdom of God.

And he took them up in his arms, put *his* hands upon them, and blessed them.  Mark 10 : 13, 14, 16.

*Hymn.*—I think when I read that sweet story of old.  Page 20.

**Q. 14.** *When did children sing the praises of Jesus when he was upon earth?*

A.  And when the chief priests and scribes saw the wonderful things that he did, and the children crying in the temple, and saying, Hosanna to the Son of David; they were sore displeased.  Matthew 21 : 15.

*Hymn.*—In days of old when Christ the Lord.  Page 188.

**Q. 15.** *What command did Jesus give to his disciples when eating the last supper with them?*

A. The Lord Jesus, the *same* night in which he was betrayed, took bread:

And when he had given thanks, he brake *it*, and said, Take, eat; this is my body, which is broken for you: this do in remembrance of me.

After the same manner also *he took* the cup, when he had supped, saying, This cup is the new testament in my blood: this do ye, as oft as ye drink *it*, in remembrance of me. 1 Corinthians 11: 23–25.

*Hymn.*—According to thy gracious word. Page 41.

Q. 16. *Who betrayed Jesus into the hands of his enemies?*

A. Then one of the twelve, called Judas Iscariot, went unto the chief priests,

And said *unto them*, What will ye give me, and I will deliver him unto you? And they covenanted with him for thirty pieces of silver. Matthew 26: 14, 15.

*Hymn.*—I lay my sins on Jesus. Page 39.

Q. 17. *To what place did Jesus go with his disciples at night, after the last supper?*

A. And he came out, and went, as he was wont, to the mount of Olives; and his disciples also followed him.

And he was withdrawn from them about a stone's cast, and kneeled down, and prayed,

Saying, Father, if thou be willing, remove this cup from me: nevertheless, not my will, but thine, be done.

And there appeared an angel unto him from heaven, strengthening him.

And being in an agony he prayed more earnestly: and his sweat was as it were great drops of blood falling down to the ground. Luke 22: 39, 41–44.

*Hymn.*—Saviour! when in dust to thee. Page 80.

**Q. 18.** *How did Judas deliver Jesus up to his enemies?*

A. And while he yet spake, lo, Judas, one of the twelve, came, and with him a great multitude with swords and staves, from the chief priests and elders of the people.

Now he that betrayed him gave them a sign, saying, Whomsoever I shall kiss, that same is he; hold him fast.

And forthwith he came to Jesus, and said, Hail, Master; and kissed him. . . .

Then came they, and laid hands on Jesus, and took him. Matthew 26 : 47–50.

*Hymn.*—My faith looks up to thee. Page 42.

**Q. 19.** *In what manner was Jesus put to death by his enemies?*

A. And the whole multitude of them arose, and led him unto Pilate.

And Pilate gave sentence that it should be as they required.

He delivered Jesus to their will.

And as they led him away, they laid hold upon one Simon, a Cyrenian, coming out of the country, and on him they laid the cross, that he might bear it after Jesus.

And when they were come to the place, which is called Calvary, there they crucified him, and the malefactors, one on the right hand, and the other on the left.

And they parted his raiment, and cast lots.

And it was about the sixth hour, and there was a darkness over all the earth until the ninth hour.

And the sun was darkened, and the vail of the temple was rent in the midst. ·

And when Jesus had cried with a loud voice, he said, Father, into thy hands I commend my spirit: and having said thus, he gave up the ghost. Luke 23: 1, 24, 25, 26, 33, 34, 44, 45, 46.

But one of the soldiers with a spear pierced his side, and forthwith came there out blood and water. John 19: 34.

*Hymn.*—Alas! and did my Saviour bleed.  Page 20.

Q. 20.  *Where was the dead body of Jesus laid?*

A.  When the even was come, there came a rich man of Arimathea, named Joseph, who also himself was Jesus' disciple:

He went to Pilate, and begged the body of Jesus. Then Pilate commanded the body to be delivered. Matthew 27: 57, 58.

And there came also Nicodemus, (which at the first came to Jesus by night,) and brought a mixture of myrrh and aloes, about a hundred pound *weight*. John 19: 39.

And when Joseph had taken the body, he wrapped it in a clean linen cloth,

And laid it in his own new tomb, which he had hewn out in the rock: and he rolled a great stone to the door of the sepulchre, and departed. Matthew 27: 59, 60.

*Hymn.*—Rock of Ages, cleft for me.  Page 39.

Q. 21.  *What did the enemies of Jesus do to prevent his body being stolen from the tomb?*

A.  They went, and made the sepulchre sure, sealing the stone, and setting a watch. Matthew 27: 66.

*Hymn.*—Christ the Lord is risen to-day.  Page 145.

Q. 22.  *When did Jesus rise from the dead?*

A. In the end of the Sabbath, as it began to dawn toward the first *day* of the week, came Mary Magdalene and the other Mary to see the sepulchre.

And, behold, there was a great earthquake: for the angel of the Lord descended from heaven, and came and rolled back the stone from the door, and sat upon it.

His countenance was like lightning, and his raiment white as snow:

And for fear of him the keepers did shake, and became as dead *men*.

And the angel answered and said unto the women, Fear not ye: for I know that ye seek Jesus, which was crucified.

He is not here: for he is risen, as he said. Come see the place where the Lord lay. Matthew 28: 1–6.

*Hymn.*—I know that my Redeemer lives. Page 154.

Q. 23. *For how long a time was Jesus seen by his disciples after his resurrection from the dead?*

A. To whom also he showed himself alive after his passion by many infallible proofs, being seen of them forty days, and speaking of the things pertaining to the kingdom of God. Acts 1: 3.

*Hymn.*—We love to sing of Jesus. Page 200.

Q. 24. *Will you mention some of the occasions when Jesus was seen after his resurrection?*

A. But Mary stood without at the sepulchre weeping: and as she wept, she stooped down, *and looked* into the sepulchre,

And seeth two angels in white sitting, the one at the head, and the other at the feet, where the body of Jesus had lain.

And they say unto her, Woman, why weepest thou? She saith unto them, Because they have taken away my Lord, and I know not where they have laid him.

And when she had thus said, she turned herself back, and saw Jesus standing, and knew not that it was Jesus.

Jesus saith unto her, Mary. She turned herself, and saith unto him, Rabboni; which is to say, Master. John 20: 11–14, 16.

*Hymn.*—Mary to her Saviour's tomb. Page 153.

Then the same day at evening, being the first *day* of the week, when the doors were shut where the disciples were assembled for fear of the Jews, *came Jesus* and stood in the midst, and saith unto them, Peace *be* unto you.

And when he had so said, he shewed unto them *his* hands and his side. Then were the disciples glad, when they saw the Lord. John 20: 19, 20.

But Thomas, one of the twelve, called Didymus, was not with them when Jesus came.

The other disciples therefore said unto him, We have seen the Lord. But he said unto them, Except I shall see in his hands the print of the nails, and put my finger into the print of the nails, and thrust my hand into his side, I will not believe.

And after eight days again his disciples were within, and Thomas with them: *then* came Jesus, the doors being shut, and stood in the midst, and said, Peace be unto you.

Then saith he to Thomas, Reach hither thy finger, and behold my hands; and reach hither thy hand, and thrust *it* into my side; and be not faithless, but believing.

And Thomas answered and said unto him, My Lord and my God.  John 20 : 24–28.

*Hymn.*—Jesus' voice my name is calling.  Page 28.

Q. 25. *What command did Jesus give to his disciples before he ascended to heaven?*
A.  Go ye into all the world, and preach the gospel to every creature.  Mark 16 : 15.
And, behold, I send the promise of my Father upon you: but tarry ye in the city of Jerusalem, until ye be endued with power from on high.  Luke 24 : 49.

*Hymn.*—Go forth, ye heralds! in my name.  Page 101.

Q. 26. *From what spot did Jesus ascend to heaven?*
A.  And he led them out as far as to Bethany, and he lifted up his hands, and blessed them.
And it came to pass, while he blessed them, he was parted from them, and carried up into heaven.  Luke 24 : 50, 51.

*Hymn.*—Our Lord is risen from the dead.  Page 145.

Q. 27. *Who now appeared to the disciples?*
A.  And while they looked steadfastly toward heaven as he went up, behold, two men stood by them in white apparel;
Which also said, Ye men of Galilee, why stand ye gazing up into heaven? this same Jesus, which is taken up from you into heaven, shall so come in like manner as ye have seen him go into heaven.  Acts 1 : 10, 11.

*Hymn.*—Come, Holy Spirit, heavenly Dove.  Page 90.

**Q. 28.** *When did Jesus fulfill his promise to send the Holy Spirit upon his disciples?*

A. And when the day of Pentecost was fully come, they were all with one accord in one place.

And suddenly there came a sound from heaven as of a rushing mighty wind, and it filled all the house where they were sitting.

And there appeared unto them cloven tongues like as of fire, and it sat upon each of them.

And they were all filled with the Holy Ghost, and began to speak with other tongues, as the Spirit gave them utterance. Acts 2 : 1–4.

*Hymn.*—He's come! let every knee be bent. Page 90.

**Q. 29.** *What will the Holy Spirit do for us?*

A. A new heart also will I give you, and a new spirit will I put within you: and I will take away the stony heart out of your flesh, and I will give you an heart of flesh. Ezekiel 36 : 26.

*Hymn.*—Holy Ghost, with light divine. Page 91.

**Q. 30.** *Does God wish children to love and serve him?*

A. Remember now thy Creator in the days of thy youth. Ecclesiastes 12 : 1.

I love them that love me; and those that seek me early shall find me. Proverbs 8 : 17.

Even a child is known by his doings, whether his work *be* pure, and whether *it be* right. Proverbs 20 : 11.

*Hymn.*—Little children, come to Jesus. Page 33.

**Q. 31.** *How did Jesus show his love to us?*

A. Christ also hath loved us, and hath given himself for us an offering and a sacrifice to God. Ephesians 5 : 2.

Greater love hath no man than this, that a man lay down his life for his friends. John 15 : 13.

*Hymn.*—I love to hear the story. Page 194.

Q. 32. *How can our souls be cleansed from sin?*

A. With the precious blood of Christ, as of a lamb without blemish and without spot. 1 Peter 1 : 19.

The blood of Jesus Christ his Son cleanseth us from all sin. 1 John 1 : 7.

*Hymn.*—There is a fountain filled with blood. Page 40.

Q. 33. *What must we do to obtain salvation?*

A. Believe on the Lord Jesus Christ, and thou shalt be saved. Acts 16 : 31.

Repent ye therefore, and be converted, that your sins may be blotted out. Acts 3 : 19.

For godly sorrow worketh repentance to salvation not to be repented of. 2 Corinthians 7 : 10.

*Hymn.*—If Jesus Christ was sent. Page 37.

Q. 34. *With what does Jesus clothe those who believe on him?*

A. I will greatly rejoice in the LORD, my soul shall be joyful in my God; for he hath clothed me with the garments of salvation, he hath covered me with the robe of righteousness. Isaiah 61 : 10.

*Hymn.*—Jesus, thy blood and righteousness. Page 38.

Q. 35. *Has the Lord promised to hear us if we call upon him for these things?*

A. Ask, and it shall be given you; seek, and ye

shall find; knock, and it shall be opened unto you. Matthew 7 : 7.

Him that cometh to me I will in no wise cast out. John 6 : 37.

Verily, verily, I say unto you, Whatsoever ye shall ask the Father in my name, he will give *it* you. John 16 : 23.

*Hymn.*—Just as I am, without one plea. Page 43.

Q. 36. *How do we know that Jesus Christ is the Son of God?*

A. The Holy Ghost descended in a bodily shape like a dove upon him, and a voice came from heaven, which said, Thou art my beloved Son; in thee I am well pleased. Luke 3 : 22.

And declared *to be* the Son of God with power, according to the Spirit of holiness, by the resurrection from the dead. Romans 1 : 4.

*Hymn.*—Come, let us join our cheerful songs. Page 163.

Q. 37. *What does Jesus call himself in the Bible?*

A. I am the light of the world: he that followeth me shall not walk in darkness, but shall have the light of life. John 8 : 12.

*Hymn.*—I heard the voice of Jesus say. Page 34.

Q. 38. *Who is the* bread *and* water *of life?*

A. Jesus said unto them, I am the bread of life: he that cometh to me shall never hunger; and he that believeth on me shall never thirst. John 6 : 35.

If any man thirst, let him come unto me, and drink. John 7 : 37.

*Hymn.*—Jesus, the water of life will give. Page 31.

Q. 39. *What else does Jesus call himself?*

A. I am the good shepherd: the good shepherd giveth his life for the sheep. John 10:11.

*Hymn.*—See, the kind Shepherd, Jesus, stands. Page 30.

Q. 40. *What are God's two great commandments, in which the whole of the Ten Commandments are included?*

A. Thou shalt love the Lord thy God with all thy heart, and with all thy soul, and with all thy mind, and with all thy strength: this *is* the first commandment.

And the second *is* like, *namely* this, Thou shalt love thy neighbour as thyself. Mark 12:30, 31.

*Hymn.*—A sinner, Lord, behold I stand. Page 83.

Q. 41. *What is the Golden Rule?*

A. All things whatsoever ye would that men should do to you, do ye even so to them. Matthew 7:12.

Q. 42. *What does it teach us?*

A. This is my commandment, That ye love one another, as I have loved you. John 15:12.

Even Christ pleased not himself. Romans 15:3.

Bear ye one another's burdens, and so fulfill the law of Christ. Galatians 6:2.

Rejoice with them that do rejoice, and weep with them that weep. Romans 12:15.

*Hymn.*—To do to others as I would. Page 66.

*Repeat the First Commandment.*

A. Thou shalt have no other gods before me. Exodus 20:3.

*Repeat the Second Commandment.*

A. Thou shalt not make unto thee any graven image, or any likeness *of any thing* that *is* in heaven above, or that *is* in the earth beneath, or that *is* in the water under the earth:

Thou shalt not bow down thyself to them, nor serve them: for I the Lord thy God *am* a jealous God, visiting the iniquity of the fathers upon the children unto the third and fourth *generation* of them that hate me;

And shewing mercy unto thousands of them that love me, and keep my commandments. Exodus 20: 4–6.

Q. 43. *What is the Third Commandment?*

A. Thou shalt not take the name of the LORD thy God in vain: for the LORD will not hold him guiltless that taketh his name in vain. Exodus 20 : 7.

Q. 44. *What does it mean?*

A. Above all things, my brethren, swear not, neither by heaven, neither by the earth, neither by any other oath. James 5 : 12.

Ye shall not swear by my name falsely, neither shalt thou profane the name of thy God: I *am* the LORD. Leviticus 19 : 12.

Neither shalt thou swear by thy head, because thou canst not make one hair white or black. Matthew 5 : 36.

*Hymn.*—Words are things of little cost. Page 71.

Q. 45. *What is the Fourth Commandment?*

A. Remember the Sabbath day, to keep it holy. Six days shalt thou labor, and do all thy work:

But the seventh day *is* the Sabbath of the LORD thy God; *in it* thou shalt not do any work, thou, nor thy son, nor thy daughter, thy manservant, nor thy maidservant, nor thy cattle, nor any stranger that *is* within thy gates:

For *in* six days the LORD made heaven and earth, the sea, and all that in them *is*, and rested the seventh day: wherefore the LORD blessed the Sabbath day, and hallowed it. Exodus 20 : 8–11.

Q. 46. *What does God wish us to do on the Sabbath day?*

A. Ye shall keep my Sabbaths, and reverence my sanctuary. Leviticus 19 : 30.

God blessed the seventh day, and sanctified it. Genesis 2 : 3.

*Hymn.*—How sweet is the Sabbath, the morning of rest. Page 50.

Q. 47. *What is the Fifth Commandment?*

A. Honour thy father and thy mother: that thy days may be long upon the land which the LORD thy God giveth thee. Exodus 20 : 12.

Q. 48. *What does it mean?*

A. Children, obey *your* parents in all things: for this is well pleasing unto the Lord. Colossians 3 : 20.

Children, obey your parents in the Lord: for this is right. Ephesians 6 : 1.

*Hymn.*—The Author of salvation. Page 45.

Q. 49. *What is the Sixth Commandment?*
A. Thou shalt not kill. Exodus 20 : 13.

Q. 50. *How may we break this Commandment without putting any one to death?*

A. Whosoever hateth his brother is a murderer. 1 John 3 : 15.

Q. 51. *Is anger sinful?*

A. Be not hasty in thy spirit to be angry. Ecclesiastes 7 : 9.

*He that is* slow to anger *is* better than the mighty; and he that ruleth his spirit than he that taketh a city. Proverbs 16 : 32.

*Hymn.*—I want to be like Jesus. Page 44.

Q. 52. *Does God command us to forgive those who have injured us?*

A. Be ye kind one to another, tenderhearted, forgiving one another, even as God for Christ's sake hath forgiven you. Ephesians 4 : 32.

Forbearing one another, and forgiving one another, if any man have a quarrel against any. Colossians 3 : 13.

But if ye forgive not men their trespasses, neither will your Father forgive your trespasses. Matthew 6 : 15.

Love your enemies, bless them that curse you, do good to them that hate you, and pray for them which despitefully use you, and persecute you. Matthew 5 : 44.

*Hymn.*—Whene'er my angry passions rise. Page 47.

*Repeat the Seventh Commandment.*

A. Thou shalt not commit adultery. Exodus 20 : 14.

*Repeat the Eighth Commandment.*

A. Thou shalt not steal. Exodus 20 : 15.

Q. 53. *What does God say about stealing?*

A. Let him that stole steal no more: but rather

let him labor, working with *his* hands the thing which is good. Ephesians 4 : 28.
Ye shall not steal, neither deal falsely. Leviticus 19 : 11.

*Repeat the Ninth Commandment.*

A. Thou shalt not bear false witness against thy neighbour. Exodus 20 : 16.

Q. 54. *What does God say about* lying?
A. Lying lips *are* abomination to the LORD: but they that deal truly *are* his delight. Proverbs 12 : 22.
The lip of truth shall be established for ever: but a lying tongue *is* but for a moment. Proverbs 12 : 19.
*He that* speaketh lies shall not escape. Proverbs 19 : 5.

*Hymn.*—God is in Heaven—can he hear. Page 87.

Q. 55. *What is the Tenth Commandment?*
A. Thou shalt not covet thy neighbour's house, thou shalt not covet thy neighbour's wife, nor his manservant, nor his maidservant, nor his ox, nor his ass, nor any thing that *is* thy neighbour's. Exodus 20 : 17.

Q. 56. *What is said in the Bible about covetousness?*
A. Take heed, and beware of covetousness. Luke 12 : 15.
*Let your* conversation *be* without covetousness; *and be* content with such things as ye have. Hebrews 13 : 5.

*Hymn.*—One God I must worship supreme. Page 52.

Q. 57. *Who is constantly tempting us to sin?*

A. The devil, as a roaring lion, walketh about, seeking whom he may devour. 1 Peter 5:8.

Q. 58. *What must we do when tempted?*
A. Watch and pray, that ye enter not into temptation. Matthew 26:41.
Resist the devil, and he will flee from you. James 4:7.

Q. 59. *How can Jesus help us when we are tempted?*
A. For in that he himself hath suffered being tempted, he is able to succor them that are tempted. Hebrews 2:18.

*Hymn.*—My soul, be on thy guard. Page 76.

Q. 60. *In whom must we put our trust in all times of danger?*
A. Whoso putteth his trust in the LORD shall be safe. Proverbs 29:25.
What time I am afraid, I will trust in thee. Psalm 56:3.
Thou *art* my hiding place and my shield: I hope in thy word. Psalm 119:114.

*Hymn.*—Abide with me! fast falls the eventide. Page 199.

Q. 61. *Has the Lord promised to help us?*
A. He shall cover thee with his feathers, and under his wings shalt thou trust. Psalm 91:4.
He giveth power to the faint; and to *them that have* no might he increaseth strength. Isaiah 40:29.
O taste and see that the LORD *is* good: blessed *is* the man *that* trusteth in him. Psalm 34:8.

*Hymn.*—Nearer, my God, to thee. Page 84.

Q. 62. *What should we do for others, when Christ has done so much for us?*

A. Freely ye have received, freely give. Matthew 10:8.

That repentance and remission of sins should be preached in his name among all nations. Luke 24:47.

*Hymn.*—I've thought of little children. Page 98.

Q. 63. *What are we told in the Bible about that beautiful home which God has prepared for all who love Jesus?*

A. There shall be no night there; and they need no candle, neither light of the sun; for the Lord God giveth them light. Revelation 22:5.

They shall hunger no more, neither thirst any more; neither shall the sun light on them, nor any heat.

For the Lamb which is in the midst of the throne shall feed them, and shall lead them unto living fountains of waters: and God shall wipe away all tears from their eyes. Revelation 7:16, 17.

And there shall be no more death, neither sorrow, nor crying, neither shall there be any more pain: for the former things are passed away. Revelation 21:4.

*Hymn.*—Around the throne of God in heaven. Page 95.

### EIGHTH PSALM.

O LORD our Lord, how excellent *is* thy name in all the earth! who has set thy glory above the heavens.

Out of the mouth of babes and sucklings hast thou ordained strength because of thine enemies, that thou mightest still the enemy and the avenger.

When I consider thy heavens, the work of thy fingers, the moon and the stars, which thou hast ordained;

What is man, that thou are mindful of him? and the son of man, that thou visitest him?

For thou hast made him a little lower than the angels, and hast crowned him with glory and honor.

Thou madest him to have dominion over the works of thy hands; thou hast put all *things* under his feet:

All sheep and oxen, yea, and the beasts of the field;

The fowl of the air, and the fish of the sea, *and whatsoever* passeth through the paths of the seas.

O LORD our Lord, how excellent *is* thy name in all the earth!

*Hymn.*—Glory to the Father give.  Page 200.

## Anti-Tobacco Pledge.

With all my might and all my main,
I hereby promise to abstain
From *cigarettes*, *cigars* and *snuff*,
And all kinds of *tobacco stuff*.

*Tobacco-using* injures *health*,
And *hinders* in the way to wealth;
If *tall* and *strong*, I want to grow,
This ugly weed I must not know.

That friends of mine this pledge may choose
I will my best endeavors use;
And they, and I, will ever try,
*Tobacco's power* to defy.

M. D. STERLING.

## Anti-Cigarette Pledge.

God being my helper, I do hereby PLEDGE MYSELF, upon HONOR, to ABSTAIN from SMOKING CIGARETTES, or USING TOBACCO IN ANY FORM, and to use my influence, and BEST ENDEAVORS to INDUCE OTHERS to do the same.

# Temperance Bible Texts.

To be used in connection with any of the Temperance Hymns.

---

WATCH and pray, that ye enter not into temptation.  Matt. 26:41.

Be sober, be vigilant; because your adversary the devil, as a roaring lion, walketh about, seeking whom he may devour.  1 Peter 5:8.

Resist the devil, and he will flee from you.  James 4:7.

My son, if sinners entice thee, consent thou not.  Proverbs 1:10.

Enter not into the path of the wicked, and go not in the way of evil *men*.  Proverbs 4:14.

Even a child is known by his doings, whether his work *be* pure, and whether *it be* right.  Proverbs 20:11.

In that he himself hath suffered being tempted, he is able to succour them that are tempted.  Hebrews 2:18.

Wine *is* a mocker, strong drink *is* raging: and whosoever is deceived thereby is not wise.  Proverbs 20:1.

Woe unto them that rise up early in the morning, *that* they may follow strong drink; that continue until night, *till* wine inflame them.  Isaiah 5:11.

The drunkard and the glutton shall come to poverty.  Prov. 23:21.

Who hath woe? who hath sorrow? who hath contentions? who hath babbling? who hath wounds without cause? who hath redness of eyes?

They that tarry long at the wine; they that go to seek mixed wine.

At the last it biteth like a serpent, and stingeth like an adder. Proverbs 23 : 29, 30, 32.

Nor drunkards, nor revilers, nor extortioners, shall inherit the kingdom of God. 1 Corinthians 6 : 10.

Ponder the path of thy feet, and let all thy ways be established. Proverbs 4 : 26.

Blessed *is* the man that walketh not in the counsel of the ungodly, nor standeth in the way of sinners. Psalms 1 : 1.

Watch ye therefore, and pray always. Luke 21 : 36.

Pray that ye enter not into temptation. Luke 22 : 40.

Neither give place to the devil. Ephesians 4 : 27.

Be not among winebibbers. Proverbs 23 : 20.

Woe unto *them that are* mighty to drink wine, and men of strength to mingle strong drink. Isaiah 5 : 22.

Order my steps in thy word: and let not any iniquity have dominion over me. Psalm 119 : 133.

# INDEX.

First lines of Hymns in Roman type. First lines of Recitations in *Italics*.

                                                    HYMN

### A

| | |
|---|---|
| Abide with me, | 234 |
| According to Thy gracious word, | 46 |
| Alas! and did my Saviour bleed, | 23 |
| A little song for Jesus, | 226 |
| All over the valleys, | 8 |
| All the bells are sweet with music, | 188 |
| Almighty God, Thy piercing eye, | 99 |
| And there were in the same country, | 139 |
| Anti-Cigarette Pledge, | Page 224 |
| Anti-Tobacco Pledge, | Page 224 |
| *A pledge we make*, | 68 |
| *A recitation*. | 63 |
| Around the throne of God in heaven, | 115 |
| A sinner, Lord, behold I stand, | 97 |
| A star shone in the heavens, | 143 |
| As the buds their leaves unfolding, | 5 |
| As the soft, departing rays, | 89 |
| Away from the dusty highway, | 69 |

### B

| | |
|---|---|
| Banish gloom and sadness, | 157 |
| *Begin the day with God*, | 211 |
| Brightly gleams our banner, | 213 |

### C

| | |
|---|---|
| *Charity suffereth long, etc.*, | 79 |
| Cheerily, cheerily sing once more, | 162 |
| Cheerily hail the Christmas morn, | 144 |
| Children, to the risen Saviour, | 187 |
| Christ the Lord is risen to-day, | 174 |
| Christ was born in Bethlehem, | 159 |
| Clock Texts, | 233 |
| Come all ye little children, | 70 |
| Come children come, join. | 65 |
| Come, Holy Spirit, heavenly Dove, | 108 |
| Come, let us join, | 196 |
| Come to Jesus. | 28 |
| Commandment Hymn, | 59 |

## D

| | HYMN |
|---|---|
| Dear little children, please give, | 137 |
| Don't drink it, boys, | 66 |
| Do unto others what we would expect, | 74 |

## F

| | |
|---|---|
| Far out upon the prairie, | 123 |
| From sinful words I must refrain, | 60 |
| From the cross on Calvary's mountain, | 184 |

## G

| | |
|---|---|
| Gather, children, gather, | 171 |
| Give, said the little stream, | 134 |
| Give to Jesus, | 136 |
| Gleam out, oh, Christmas brightness, | 150 |
| Glory, glory, hallelujah, | 227 |
| Glory, glory to the Father, | 238 |
| Glory in the highest, | 169 |
| Glory to the Father give, | 236 |
| God be with you, | 231 |
| Go forth, ye heralds! in My name, | 121 |
| God is in Heaven, can He hear, | 104 |
| God made the sky that looks so blue, | 197 |
| Good news for little children, | 35 |

## H

| | |
|---|---|
| Hail to the morn, | 149 |
| Hark, I hear the angel voices, | 161 |
| Hark! I hear the Saviour calling, | 27 |
| Hark! the angels singing, | 148 |
| Hark! the merry, merry bells, | 142 |
| Have you ever brought a penny, | 124 |
| Hear the pennies dropping, | 127 |
| He is coming! He is coming, | 158 |
| Here are joyous faces, | 223 |
| Here's a lesson all should heed, | 83 |
| He's come! let ev'ry knee be bent, | 109 |
| *He shall build a house for my name*, | 208 |
| Holy Bible, | 1 |
| Holy Ghost, with light divine, | 110 |
| How loving is Jesus who came, | 15 |
| How precious is the story, | 21 |
| How sweet is the Sabbath, | 58 |

## I

| | |
|---|---|
| I am a little Hindoo girl, | 125 |
| I am a little soldier, | 218 |
| I am but a penny, | 122 |
| I am singing, singing, | 222 |
| I am so young, O Jesus, | 199 |

## INDEX.

|  | HYMN |
|---|---|
| I asked the little joyous bird, | 195 |
| *I believe in God the Father,* | 91 |
| *I believe in God the Father.* | 237 |
| I cannot do great things for God, | 133 |
| If Jesus Christ was sent, | 41 |
| I heard the voice of Jesus say, | 37 |
| I hear the voices of children, | 120 |
| I know that my Redeemer lives, | 186 |
| I lay my sins on Jesus, | 44 |
| I love Thee, Jesus, | 107 |
| I love to hear the story, | 230 |
| In a country far away, | 154 |
| In days of old when Christ the Lord, | 221 |
| In the ways of true temperance, | 64 |
| Into her chamber went, | 98 |
| I ought to be a happy child, | 12 |
| I promise Thee, sweet Lord. | 73 |
| I sing the mighty power of God, | 11 |
| I think when I read that sweet story, | 22 |
| It is God's mercy, | 10 |
| It is not far to Jesus, | 26 |
| I've thought of little children, | 118 |
| I've two little hands to work, | 204 |
| I want to be an angel, | 112 |
| I want to be like Jesus, | 49 |
| I was but a little lamb, | 85 |

### J

| Jesus invites you, oh, do not delay, | 228 |
|---|---|
| Jesus is knocking, | 32 |
| Jesus, lover of my soul, | 105 |
| Jesus loves me, | 24 |
| Jesus, Saviour, pity me, | 94 |
| Jesus, tender Shepherd, | 103 |
| Jesus, the water of life will give, | 34 |
| Jesus, Thy blood and righteousness, | 42 |
| Jesus' voice my name is calling, | 31 |
| Jesus, when a little child, | 50 |
| Just as I am, | 48 |

### K

| Keeping step with Jesus, | 220 |
|---|---|

### L

| Let ev'ry childish voice, | 177 |
|---|---|
| Lifting up each chalice bright, | 7 |
| Lift up, O little children. | 180 |
| Lift up your faces o'er hill and vale, | 224 |
| *Lift up your hands in the sanctuary,* | 212 |

# INDEX.

|  | HYMN |
|---|---|
| List, a thousand birds are singing, | 170 |
| List to the bells of Christmas, | 140 |
| Little builders all are we, | 119 |
| Little children, can you tell, | 151 |
| Little children, come to Jesus, | 36 |
| Little children love each other, | 75 |
| Little drops of water, | 191 |
| Little gentle breath, | 202 |
| Little hands are clapping now, | 189 |
| Little knees should lowly bend, | 205 |
| Long, long ago, | 141 |
| Lord, a little tired child, | 39 |
| Lord Jesus, I long to be perfectly whole, | 96 |
| *Lord, teach a little child,* | 201 |
| Low in the grave He lay, | 178 |

## M

| Mary to her Saviour's tomb, | 185 |
|---|---|
| Merry Christmas bells are ringing, | 165 |
| Merry, merry Christmas, | 153 |
| More like Jesus, | 54 |
| Mourn for the thousands slain, | 67 |
| My faith looks up to Thee, | 47 |
| My soul, be on thy guard, | 87 |

## N

| Nearer, my God, to Thee, | 100 |
|---|---|
| Never be afraid, | 84 |
| Now I lay me down to sleep, | 93 |
| Now the bursting Spring awakes, | 179 |
| Now who are these, whose little feet, | 214 |

## O

| Of all the tints the light looks on, | 62 |
|---|---|
| Oh, how brightly, | 192 |
| Oh, many, many children, | 29 |
| Oh, send forth the Bible, | 128 |
| Oh, tell us how our bread is made, | 198 |
| Oh, the sweet, sweet words of Jesus, | 77 |
| O joyful bells of Christmas-tide, | 146 |
| One God I must worship supreme, | 59 |
| One step and then another, | 82 |
| One there is above all others, | 20 |
| Only a single penny, | 131 |
| Only little children, | 14 |
| On this glad triumphant morning, | 176 |
| On this happy day we gather, | 225 |
| On this our glad birthday, | 229 |
| O sing to me of Jesus, | 13 |

|  | HYMN |
|---|---|
| Our Father who in heaven art, | 101 |
| Our Father, which art in heaven, | 102 |
| Our Heav'nly King from His throne, | 78 |
| Our Lord is risen from the dead, | 175 |
| Out in the western wild, | 130 |
| Over the ocean wave, | 116 |

**P**

| | |
|---|---|
| Precious Bible! how I love thee, | 2 |

**Q**

| | |
|---|---|
| Questions and answers, | 25 |

**R**

| | |
|---|---|
| Ring, Sabbath bells. | 57 |
| Ring the bells, the Christmas bells, | 155 |
| Rise up, rise up so promptly, | 207 |
| Rock of Ages, | 43 |
| Round our sparkling Christmas tree, | 145 |

**S**

| | |
|---|---|
| Safe in the arms of Jesus, | 113 |
| Saviour! when in dust to Thee. | 92 |
| See, the kind Shepherd Jesus stands, | 33 |
| Should you wish to be told, | 126 |
| Shout, shout aloud the tidings, | 172 |
| Sing a song of jugs to-night, | 129 |
| Snowdrops lift your timid heads, | 182 |
| Softly sing the love of Jesus. | 18 |
| Softly, softly through the midnight, | 138 |
| *Softly whisper, softly speak,* | 90 |
| Sound the battle cry, | 217 |
| Summer days, | 9 |
| Sweet Easter bells are ringing, | 183 |

**T**

| | |
|---|---|
| Tell me why is Christmas day, | 167 |
| Temperance Bible Texts, | Page 225. |
| Ten Commandments, | Page 51. |
| Texts arranged alphabetically, | 232 |
| The anthem the angels were singing, | 147 |
| The Author of salvation, | 51 |
| The bells are merrily ringing, | 181 |
| The church of God through ages past, | 209 |
| The deadly cup, | 61 |
| The foxes have their dwelling. | 52 |
| The little flowers came from the ground, | 173 |
| *The Lord has made me, yet sometimes,* | 203 |
| The morning bright with rosy light, | 106 |
| The pretty flow'rs have come again, | 6 |

|  | HYMN |
|---|---|
| *There a boy (perhaps you),* | 63 |
| There is a fountain filled with blood. | 45 |
| There is a happy land, | 111 |
| There is beauty all around. | 80 |
| There is something on earth, | 132 |
| There's a Friend for little children. | 16 |
| There's a land that is fairer than day, | 114 |
| The snow comes down so pure, | 190 |
| They crowned our Saviour's brow, | 19 |
| This day belongs to God alone. | 55 |
| Tho' dark the night, and clouds, | 40 |
| Though I am a little child, | 219 |
| Through the blue and starry heavens, | 164 |
| Throw out the Life-line, | 117 |
| 'Tis in the Bible that we read, | 210 |
| 'Tis wonderful love in Christ we see, | 17 |
| To do to others as I would, | 76 |
| To our dear Sabbath-school, | 135 |
| Touch not the cup it is death. | 71 |
| To us this day in David's town, | 152 |
| *Two little eyes to look to God,* | 194 |

### U

| Unto us a Child is born, | 160 |
|---|---|

### W

| Wakeful shepherds, long ago, | 166 |
|---|---|
| We are coming, | 72 |
| We are little travelers, | 216 |
| We are marching to the river, | 215 |
| We'll all rise up together, | 193 |
| We'll all stand up. | 206 |
| We'll not give up the Bible, | 3 |
| We love to sing of Jesus, | 235 |
| We must not work on Sunday. | 56 |
| We saw a star, a bright new star, | 163 |
| What do we find in the manger, | 168 |
| *What says the clock,* | 200 |
| What tender words! how sweet a voice, | 30 |
| When'er my angry passions rise, | 53 |
| When'er you see a schoolboy, | 86 |
| When little Samuel woke, | 38 |
| While shepherds watched their flocks, | 156 |
| Who made the sky so bright and blue? | 4 |
| When daily I kneel down to pray, | 95 |
| Words are things of little cost, | 81 |

### Y

| Yield not to temptation, | 88 |
|---|---|

www.ingramcontent.com/pod-product-compliance
Lightning Source LLC
Chambersburg PA
CBHW021819230426
43669CB00008B/799